ELIZABETH SHEE T\

IRISH MEGALITHIC TOMBS

Second edition

SHIRE ARCHAEOLOGY

Cover photograph
Brenanstown portal tomb, County Dublin.
(Photograph: author)

British Library Cataloguing in Publication Data:
Twohig, Elizabeth Shee
Irish megalithic tombs. – 2nd ed. – (Shire archaeology; 63)
1. Megalithic monuments – Ireland
2. Ireland – Antiquities
I. Title 936.1'5
ISBN 0 7478 0598 9.

Published in 2004 by
SHIRE PUBLICATIONS LTD
Cromwell House, Church Street, Princes Risborough,
Buckinghamshire HP27 9AA, UK.
(Website: www.shirebooks.co.uk)

Series Editor: James Dyer.

Number 63 in the Shire Archaeology series.

ISBN 0 7478 0598 9.

First published 1990. Second edition 2004.

Printed in Great Britain by
CIT Printing Services Ltd, Press Buildings,
Merlins Bridge, Haverfordwest, Pembrokeshire SA61 1XF.

Contents

List of illustrations

Acknowledgements

This book draws on the work of many colleagues for information and help and for permission to reproduce illustrations. I would particularly like to thank Séan Ó Nualláin, formerly of the Archaeological Branch of the Ordnance Survey, and his colleagues Eamon Cody and Paul Walsh, who are now based in the National Monuments Section, Heritage and Planning Division, Department of the Environment, Heritage and Local Government, for providing me with unpublished distribution maps. I also wish to thank Anna Brindley, Rose Cleary, George Eogan, Claire Foley, Ann Lynch and Patrick Quinlan for information and/or help and Colin Rynne for reconstruction drawings of tombs.

The following individuals and institutions kindly gave permission to reproduce illustrations: Con Brogan; Professor G. Eogan and Ms H. Richardson; C. Foley; Professor M. Herity; Dr C. Jones; Mrs C. O'Kelly; Lee Snodgrass; the late D. L. Swan; Clarendon Press, Oxford; Department of the Environment, Northern Ireland, and *Ulster Journal of Archaeology*; National Monuments Section, Heritage and Planning Division, Department of the Environment, Heritage and Local Government; Royal Irish Academy.

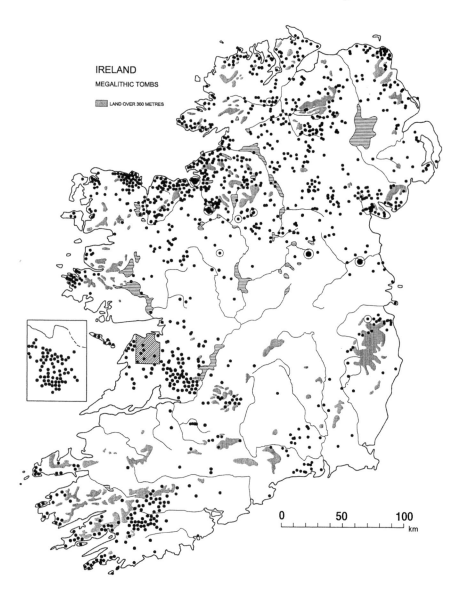

1. Distribution map of Irish megalithic tombs. A small dot indicates 1–2 sites; a small dot in a circle denotes 3–8 sites, and a large dot in a circle 9 or more sites. (2003: courtesy the National Monuments Section, Department of the Environment, Heritage and Local Government)

1
Introduction

The earliest evidence we have for human occupation in Ireland dates to about 8000 BC, and for the next four thousand years people provided for themselves by fishing, hunting and gathering wild plants. However, changes began to take place from about 4000 BC onwards, with the gradual introduction of farming bringing domesticated cereals and animals from Britain and/or northern France. Soon afterwards people began to build what we now call megalithic tombs (from the Greek *megas lithos* – 'big stone'). In Ireland just under 1600 of these monuments have been recorded. Archaeologists use the term 'Neolithic' (meaning 'New Stone Age') for this period, *c*.4000–2500/2300 BC, and some tombs continued to be built to *c*.1700 BC in the succeeding Bronze Age. Similar structures were built in many areas of western Europe at about the same time as in Ireland.

Very large stones were often used in the construction of these monuments, and the ability to manoeuvre these enormous stones has for long been a source of amazement to even the most casual observer. In Ireland, the biggest stone used in a tomb is believed to be the capstone of the tomb at Kernanstown, County Carlow, which weighs nearly 150 tonnes. Excavations have taken place at less than 10 per cent of all sites in Ireland, but these show that human remains were deposited in the monuments, generally following cremation. Pottery and stone tools were usually laid in the tombs with the burials, and there is evidence that a range of ritual practices took place at various times at these monuments.

Megalithic tombs have been excavated, surveyed and discussed over many years, but much of what has been discovered about them by archaeologists is available only in specialised or obscure publications, or in picture books with little or no accompanying text. I hope that this book will result in an improved awareness and understanding of these sites and contribute to their conservation. Even the smallest tombs are of considerable interest, and all are part of the heritage and should be properly recorded and protected. Sites are still being discovered, both by archaeological survey teams and by interested amateur archaeologists or local historians, and each tomb adds to our knowledge of the past.

Classification of monuments

Most of the sixteen hundred or so megalithic tombs now recorded in Ireland (figure 1) have been assigned to four main groups: court tombs, portal tombs, passage tombs and wedge tombs. A summary of the main characteristics of each is given here. As can be seen from the map, megalithic tombs were built over most of the country, excluding the east midlands and parts of the south and east. The totals for each category are based on information kindly supplied to me in 2003 from the records of the Archaeological Branch of the Ordnance Survey, which are now held by the National Monuments Section, Heritage and Planning Division, Department of the Environment, Heritage and Local Government. Over two hundred of the total number of sites cannot, however, be assigned to a particular type or group and are designated 'unclassified'.

The specialised terms used in describing the tombs are explained in the Glossary (page 61).

1. Court tombs (412 examples). These sites have an open court from which access is gained to a roofed gallery or burial area. This consists of two or more chambers set one behind the other. The chambers have low corbelled roofs and are enclosed in a cairn of stones, the edges of which are delimited by kerbstones or occasionally by dry-stone walling. In some regions, variations on the 'standard' plan were developed.

Court tombs occur almost exclusively in the northern part of the country. These sites are discussed fully in Chapter 3.

2. Portal tombs (180 examples). These are often quite spectacular monuments, with a single chamber covered by a large capstone. Many have two tall orthostats ('portals') set at the front of the tomb so that the capstone rises to the front, sometimes at a significant angle. They occur mainly in the northern part of Ireland, but with a considerable number also in the south-east. Portal tombs are discussed fully in Chapter 4.

3. Passage tombs (236 examples). This type of tomb has a relatively narrow passage leading to a chamber. Smaller chambers or cells frequently open off the main chamber, sometimes producing a 'cruciform' plan. The passages were roofed with capstones ('lintel' stones), as were the smaller chambers, but the larger chambers were corbelled. Many of the structural stones had designs or symbols carved on them. A round cairn covers the tomb structure, and the cairn is generally edged with kerbstones. There is considerable variation in the size of these monuments. Passage tombs tend to occur in cemeteries or groups and are sometimes sited on high ground or hilltops. The distribution is mainly in the north and east of the island. Passage tombs are discussed fully in Chapter 5.

4. Wedge tombs (543 examples). These monuments consist of a rectangular main chamber or gallery. In most examples the wider, entrance end is at the west, and there may be a straight façade of orthostats running out on each side of the entrance, marking the edge of the cairn. A 'portico' may be built at the western end of the main chamber, or, more rarely, an end chamber occurs at the eastern end. The tombs were roofed with capstones or 'lintels'. The distribution is quite widespread, with the densest concentrations to be found in Clare and in central Cork. The sites are discussed fully in Chapter 6.

5. *Other sites.* Many sites are unclassifiable because little survives of them, but excavation would probably reveal the original structure and allow them to be classified. However, the fact that at present count 215 sites are deemed 'unclassified' serves as a reminder that our current division of Irish megalithic tombs into four types is partly the consequence of the perceived requirement for archaeologists to create typologies, and we should not assume that the builders of these sites thought of them in such neat categories. It has been suggested that the term 'tradition' would more accurately describe the nature of these categories, recognising the wide variations in design morphology that can occur within a single 'type'.

Another difficulty with classifying sites is that some appear to have been altered; for example, it has been argued that the court tomb at Tamnyrankin, County Derry, had a wedge tomb added at the rear of the cairn, and the portal tomb at Drumhallagh Upper, County Donegal, seems to have been converted into a court tomb. Many sites were reused in later periods, particularly by the insertion of burials during the Bronze Age, and cairns were occasionally added to cover these new burials, again making their classification through field survey more difficult. Regional tomb traditions are also evident, such as a small number of sites in west Galway that do not fit readily into any of the four main tomb types. Their chambers may be rectangular or round in plan and they are roofed by one or two capstones. Their maximum dimension is usually 2 to 3 metres. None has yet been excavated. In the south, many sites classified as portal tombs seem never to have had a portal feature, but have a large capstone propped up over a small chamber (for example Castle Mary, County Cork, figure 2). None of these has been excavated and they may well have had a different use-history from the classic portal tomb.

Other contemporary forms of burial

During the Neolithic period people also buried their dead in pits, caves or rock crevices. In some areas they built small chambers known as 'single grave burials' or 'Linkardstown cists', usually covered by a large cairn, and generally containing only the body of a single adult male. In most areas, only a fraction of the population may have been buried in megalithic tombs, and many bodies must have been disposed of with little formality. The practice of building tombs from large stones continued in the south-west well into the Bronze Age (down to *c.*1200

2. Castle Mary, County Cork: simple portal tomb. (Photo: author)

BC or later), where small, above-ground structures known as 'boulder burials' are found. Elsewhere, during the Bronze Age, burials were placed in the ground in a slab-covered pit or box-like slab-built structure known as a 'cist'. These cists generally contain only a single burial, or at most the burials (cremated or inhumed) of a small number of people, unlike the megalithic tombs, where several people were placed in the chambers over a period of time.

Dating megalithic tombs
The application of radiocarbon dating methods for determining the chronology of megalithic tombs has confirmed a general date of *c*.3800–2800 BC for court tombs, portal tombs and passage tombs, with wedge tombs considerably later, *c*.2500–1800 BC. However, it is difficult to have much confidence in many of the dates obtained in the early days of radiocarbon dating. Most were based on charcoal, sometimes from insecure contexts, occasionally from underneath the cairn or from an amalgamation of samples. A further problem with dating charcoal is encountered if the sample comes from a big tree such as oak: the date for the bark will be much younger than for the middle of the tree (this is known as the 'old wood factor'). Furthermore, it is not possible to be

sure that the timber was cut down at the time it was incorporated into the monument. Dating of charcoal from twigs is more satisfactory, as is the use of charred grain or hazelnuts, as all of these are short-lived. Dating of bone from the burials is probably the best option, and techniques have now been developed for dating cremated bone, which should help enormously in determining the sequence of burials and deposition at megalithic tombs.

2
History of Irish megalithic tomb studies

Early literature and traditions

Many instances are recorded of an association between prehistoric tombs or mounds and the supernatural beings or gods of early Irish mythology. The best-documented is the identification (by George Petrie in 1845) of Newgrange as the *Brú na Bóinne* of early Irish literature. The name (broadly translatable as 'mansion or abode by the Boyne') occurs in many Irish records; the earliest that survives dates to the eleventh century AD, but all have their foundations in much older literature and before that, in oral traditions. Newgrange can be identified as the dwelling place of the powerful god Dagda, his wife, Boann, and son, Aonghus. It has been suggested that the belief that these were the abodes of supernatural beings may go back to the time of the construction of the tombs.

Newgrange in particular, as the home of Dagda, seems to have been specially revered and this may explain the deposition around the tomb entrance there of many valuable Roman coins and Romano-British ornaments in the fourth century AD. The nearby sites of Dowth and Knowth were used as settlement places during the early medieval period, with Knowth especially important as the seat of the kings of the territory of Northern Brega, and later passing into Cistercian ownership.

Antiquarian interest in megalithic tombs began in the late seventeenth century, and a description and sketch of the tomb at Labbacallee, County Cork, was included in John Aubrey's *Monumenta Britannica*, compiled in the 1670s. The earliest record of finds from a megalithic tomb seems to be the report to the Dublin Philosophical Society of the accidental discovery in 1685 of what we now know to be an early Bronze Age pot in a passage tomb at Waringstown, County Down.

The majority of antiquarians were ignorant of the Irish traditions and most of them ascribed the tombs and various other Irish monuments to the Danes, or even to the Phoenicians or Egyptians. It was believed that the Irish were too barbarous to have built such a sophisticated site as Newgrange, in the same way that Stonehenge was attributed to almost anyone but the native British. A notable exception was Edward Lhwyd, Keeper of Antiquities at the Ashmolean Museum, Oxford, who visited Newgrange in 1699 when it was first entered. Lhwyd's letters provide a good record of the monument, as do the drawings made by his draftsman. Lhwyd argued that it was 'some place of sacrifice of the ancient Irish', on the basis that the finding of a Roman coin in the cairn proved that the

3. Excavation of burial deposit in chamber 1, Parknabinnia, County Clare (Cl.153), in 2000. (Photo: C. Jones)

monument was 'ancienter than any invasion of the Ostmans or Danes and the carving and rude sculpture, barbarous'.

Some reports survive from the eighteenth century, but the first systematic countrywide record of archaeological sites resulted from the work of the Ordnance Survey, which was established in Ireland in 1824. A 'Place Names and Antiquities Section' was created in 1830, staffed by three distinguished scholars, George Petrie, John O'Donovan and Eugene O'Curry. O'Curry was subsequently appointed as the first Irish professor to have 'archaeology' in the title of his university post – the Chair of Irish History and Archaeology at the Catholic University in Dublin. Another associate was George V. Du Noyer, who made accurate drawings of many monuments, before photography became commonplace (figure 4). A list of megalithic tombs based on the maps was compiled under the direction of Margaret Stokes and published in the *Révue Archéologique* of Paris in 1882. More general accounts and attempts at classifying the monuments began to appear, such as James Ferguson's *Rude Stone Monuments in All Countries* (1872), and in 1897 William Copeland Borlase published *The Dolmens of Ireland* in three volumes, recording nearly nine hundred monuments.

Excavations were carried out occasionally in the nineteenth and early twentieth centuries, but they began in earnest in the 1930s, particularly in the north, where Oliver Davies and others such as Estyn Evans and Ivor Herring were very active. Funding for excavations in the Republic of Ireland became available in 1934 under the Relief of Unemployment Programme, enabling H. G. Leask and Liam Price to excavate at Labbacallee, County Cork. In the following year a large-scale excavation directed by H. O'Neill Hencken began at Creevykeel court tomb in

4. Loughcrew, County Meath: drawing *c.*1864 of interior of cairn L. (Drawing: G.V. Du Noyer; by permission of the Royal Irish Academy)

County Sligo, as part of the Harvard Archaeological Mission to Ireland. The degree of excavation activity can be seen from the large numbers of site reports published during the 1930s in periodicals such as the *Proceedings of the Belfast Natural History and Philosophical Society*, the *Ulster Journal of Archaeology*, the *Proceedings of the Royal Irish Academy* and the *Journal of the Royal Society of Antiquaries of Ireland*.

Fieldwork and surveying of sites have been undertaken at various levels. In Northern Ireland, details of many megalithic tombs were published in the *Preliminary Survey of Ancient Monuments* (1940) and in the *Archaeological Survey of County Down* (1966). In the Republic, the Archaeological Branch of the Ordnance Survey was established in 1949 to provide a survey of the megalithic tombs of Ireland. Seven volumes have been published to date, covering seventeen counties, and fieldwork has been completed for the remaining counties. However, an unfortunate early decision to omit details of the passage tombs from the individual county surveys makes for somewhat skewed coverage. The *Sites and Monuments Records* and the *Records of Monuments and Places*

5. Poulnabrone, County Clare: conservation in progress. (Photo: C. Brogan)

contain lists of monuments on a county basis, which are coupled to the Ordnance Survey six-inch maps. Fuller records of individual sites on a county basis can be found in the *Inventories* (or *Surveys*) *of Archaeological Monuments*, though all counties are not yet published.

Excavations have continued, some as part of a planned research project, for example Billy O'Brien's work at Altar and Toormore, County Cork (published 1999), while others have been undertaken because of the demands of conservation or development. Notable among the latter are M. J. O'Kelly's work at Newgrange from 1962 to 1975, Ann Lynch's 1986/1988 excavations at Poulnabrone portal tomb, County Clare (figures 5 and 15), and Claire Foley's four seasons of excavations at Creggandevesky court tomb, County Tyrone (figure 6), while Declan Hurl's publication of the rescue excavations at Ballybriest, County Derry, has improved our understanding of wedge tombs. The longest-running excavation by far has been that at Knowth, County Meath, where work began in 1962 and ended effectively forty years later with the opening of the site to the public.

3
Court tombs

The essential features of a court tomb are a long cairn (average 25–35 metres long) of trapezoidal (or occasionally rectangular or D-shaped) plan, with an unroofed court at the wider, eastern end of the cairn. The burial gallery consists of two or more chambers placed longitudinally in relation to the cairn. A range of more complex sites was also built and will be discussed below. The name 'court tomb' has been adopted to replace older terms such as 'court cairns', 'horned cairns' or 'lobster-claw cairns'.

Structure and design

The two-chambered gallery is most commonly found, with the chambers separated from each other by a pair of jamb stones, sometimes with a low sill stone between them. A number of three- or four-chambered galleries are also known (figures 6 and 7). A small antechamber is present at some sites. Subsidiary chambers occur at about 10 per cent of

6. Creggandevesky court tomb, County Tyrone, after excavation. (Crown copyright, reproduced with permission of the Controller of Her Majesty's Stationery Office)

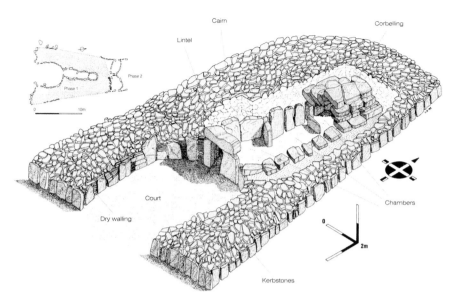

7. Annaghmare court tomb, County Armagh (after Waterman 1965).

the sites, usually opening on to the side of the cairn, but occasionally on to the rear or the court. At Annaghmare, County Armagh (figure 7), the excavator suggested that the two subsidiary chambers were added on to the end of the cairn.

The roofing of the gallery was generally by means of a lintel or capstone, which spanned the jamb stones at the chamber entrances, while the chambers proper were corbelled, with two or three rows of stones, each succeeding level extending beyond the one beneath it (figure 7).

A line of kerbstones usually defines the cairn edge (for example Annaghmare, County Armagh, figure 7), though revetments built from dry-stone walling have been found during excavations at several sites (for example at Audleystown, County Down, figure 8; and Behy, County Mayo, figure 8). In some cases walling has been recorded over the kerbstones (for example Creevykeel, County Sligo).

The orthostats forming the court are often quite tall, particularly near the entrance to the tomb. Careful excavation at Annaghmare, County Armagh, revealed panels of dry walling between some of the orthostats and over some of the lower ones (figure 7) and a completely dry-built court was recorded at Behy, County Mayo (figure 8). Open courts are most commonly found (figure 6), though a number of full-court tombs

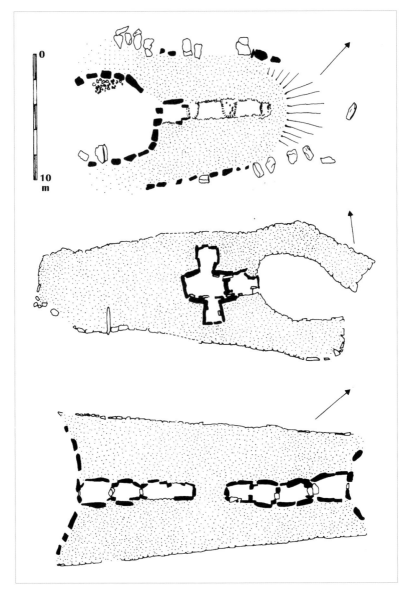

8. Court tombs at Ballymacaldrack, County Antrim (after Collins 1976); Behy, County Mayo (after de Valera 1965); and Audleystown, County Down (after Collins 1959). (By permission of the Department of the Environment, Northern Ireland, the *Ulster Journal of Archaeology*, and the Department of the Environment, Heritage and Local Government)

9. Shanballyedmond court tomb, County Tipperary. (Photo: author)

also occur, particularly around Donegal Bay (figures 10 and 11). At Creevykeel (figure 10) a change in size of the orthostats edging the court suggests that the inner part of the court might have been built first, with the outer section later.

A number of variations and elaborations of the 'typical' court-tomb plan are known. One is the dual-court tomb, where two galleries and courts of regular plan are set, as it were, back to back, and covered by a single cairn (for example Audleystown, County Down, figure 8). These are generally found in south to mid Ulster, with thirty-three definite and

10. Creevykeel court tomb, County Sligo (after Hencken 1939). (By permission of the Royal Irish Academy)

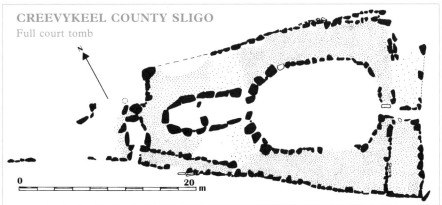

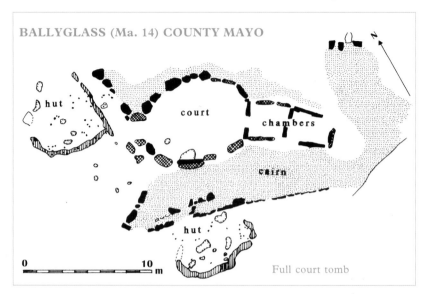

BALLYGLASS (Ma. 14) COUNTY MAYO

hut

court

chambers

cairn

hut

0   10
                        m

Full court tomb

11. Ballyglass (Mayo 14), County Mayo: court tomb and huts. (Courtesy S. Ó Nualláin)

thirteen possible examples recorded. Other elaborations of the court-tomb plan are found almost exclusively in the west, particularly around Donegal Bay. These include eight sites with a central court, and twelve sites where a small chamber or 'transept' opens off the gallery (for example, Behy, County Mayo, figure 8), possibly influenced by the 'cruciform' plan passage tombs of the area such as those at Carrowkeel, County Sligo (see Chapter 5). Two-chambered galleries were preferred in mid Ulster and the west, while four-chambered examples were built in the east.

Other regional variations have been noted such as the combination of short cairn and straight-sided courts at four sites in Counties Clare and Tipperary. At one of these, Shanballyedmond, County Tipperary (figure 9), the short cairn was completely removed during excavation to reveal a U-shaped setting of posts about 2.3 metres beyond the edge of the cairn, which may have been added to the site in the middle Bronze Age, according to the radiocarbon dates.

Distribution, topography and associations

The distribution map of the 412 court tombs now on record (figure 12) shows their occurrence almost exclusively in the northern part of the country, with only eight sites south of the line from Dundalk Bay to

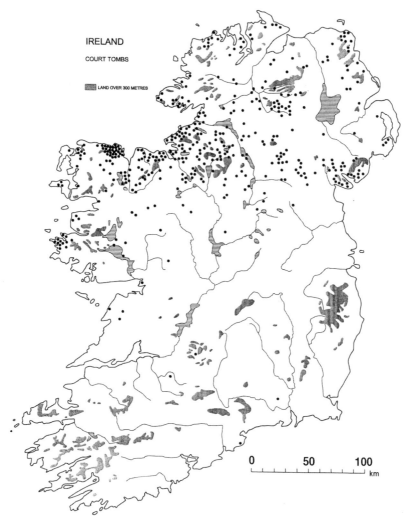

12. Map of Irish court tombs. (2003: courtesy the National Monuments Section, Department of the Environment, Heritage and Local Government)

Galway Bay. Ó Nualláin's analysis of the altitudes of the 354 known court tombs in 1983 showed that 60 per cent lay below 120 metres in altitude. Cooney has shown that in south Leitrim all types of megalithic tombs tend to concentrate on fertile land, and he has suggested that this soil was chosen because it was easily cultivated and therefore people must have been living near tombs. Settlement certainly occurred near the court tombs in north Mayo, where several megalithic tombs are recorded within field systems. Here parallel field walls were built running upslope from the coast and the strips so formed were divided by cross-walls into fields of up to 7 hectares in extent. The court tomb of Behy is sited within the extensive Céide fields complex, and near an oval habitation enclosure. Just east of Céide, at Rathlacken, Gretta Byrne has excavated a three-chambered court tomb, which is also associated with a field system; an enclosure containing a house was later added to the side of the cairn. Two court tombs at Ballyglass, County Mayo, are associated with houses. A rectangular house, 13 by 8 metres, found under one tomb (known as Mayo 13 in the Megalithic Survey) may have been demolished to make way for the tomb, while two smaller structures were found beside Mayo 14 (figure 11). The cairn at Ballybriest, County Derry, was apparently built on top of a place of habitation.

Burial practices

Excavations have been carried out at approximately fifty court tombs, though not all of the excavation reports are fully published. Excavation reveals information about the details of the structure and the uses of the tomb, such as burial practices, and it generally produces artefacts that seem to have been placed in the chambers with the human remains. There is some evidence that fires were lit in the court-tomb chambers; the floors were often paved and burials were placed on the paving and were sometimes covered over with slabs. Cremated remains are most commonly found; in some cases charcoal and clay were found mixed with the bones, as if collected from a funeral pyre. Many sites also have sherds of pottery and tools made from flint or other stone mixed in with the cremations and earth, and it has been suggested that this material was collected from settlements for deposition in the tombs. Inhumation burials also occur, but they are far less common than cremation. These may have been placed in the tomb after the cremations, because they often occur at higher levels. Usually the numbers of individuals identified are quite low, the largest yet recorded being at Audleystown, County Down, where about thirty-three individuals were found in the ratio of 1:2, cremation: inhumation. The burials were found in six of the eight chambers in the monument (figure 8), the unburnt bones being placed in little piles, and the excavator believed they had been brought into the tomb already disarticulated, having been stored elsewhere before being placed in the monument. A minimum number of twenty-one people has been reported from Creggandevesky, County Tyrone, and at least eighteen from the gallery at Parknabinnia, County Clare (figure 3).

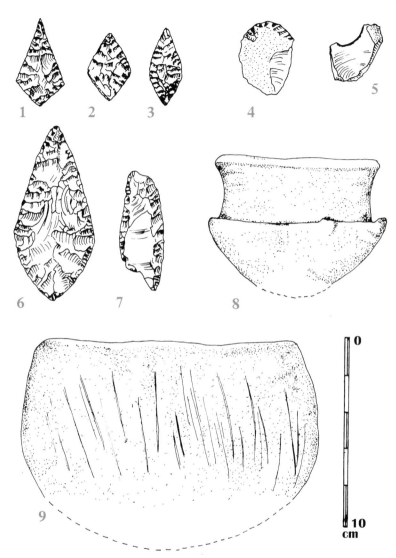

13. Artefacts from Irish court tombs: numbers 1, 2, 3, 6, 7, 8 and 9 from Audleystown, County Down (after Collins 1959); numbers 4 and 5 from Annaghmare, County Armagh (after Waterman 1965). (By permission of the Department of the Environment, Northern Ireland, and the *Ulster Journal of Archaeology*)

It seems likely that the sites remained in use for quite a long period. This suggestion is based on a study of the pottery, which shows that early Neolithic pottery (round-bottomed and without decoration) is found both in pre-cairn levels and in the (apparently) primary levels in the chambers (figure 13). Decorated pottery is believed to be of slightly later date, and neither this nor the flat-based plain pottery have been found beneath the cairns, occurring instead in the upper levels of the chambers and on the floors of the courts. After burial ceased, it appears that the tomb entrance was blocked and the area in front was sometimes filled with stones.

Flint arrowheads are frequently found in the monuments, with chert often replacing flint in the west. The arrowheads are usually very well made, as are the larger 'javelin' heads (figure 13.6). A range of scrapers and knives also occurs, and unworked or 'waste' flint. There are also stone axes or adzes, and stone beads of various forms. Quartz crystals and artefacts made from quartz were deposited at a number of sites.

Bones of cattle, sheep and some pig have been found at many sites, also some red deer and wolf or dog, and a possible bear's tooth. Some of the bones are clearly primary while others are secondary and seem to have been thrown in at the time of sealing the tomb. The animal bones are usually interpreted as indicating that funeral feasts took place, though some may be deliberately deposited. Pits, hearths and a range of pottery and other artefacts occur in the courts as well as in the chambers and show that the courts were used for ritual activities.

At Ballymacaldrack, County Antrim (figure 8), excavation in the central area of the cairn revealed three post-pits, which seem to have belonged to some sort of wooden mortuary structure or platform, possibly for cremation. A cairn seems to have been built around this, and at a later stage a chamber and court were built to the south-west of the row of pits, thus creating a small court tomb. Nothing quite like this has been found elsewhere in Ireland, but similar wooden structures are known in Britain, and further east on mainland Europe.

Many sites have been reused in a multiplicity of ways since their construction, and pottery of different periods is recorded at many sites, including early Bronze Age urns and food vessels, late Bronze Age coarse ware, souterrain ware of the early medieval period and, occasionally, medieval pottery. This degree of later activity at many megalithic tombs means that the primary material has often been disturbed, making it difficult to understand the original use of the sites.

Dating court tombs

Most of the radiocarbon dates obtained from samples at court tombs are from charcoal and may thus come from contexts older than the tombs (see Chapter 1). Apart from the dates obtained from habitation levels under court tombs (and therefore earlier than the tomb's construction), there are very few dates that can be assigned satisfactorily to the period of construction or use of the tomb. However, there are enough to date the monuments to the fourth millennium BC. Creggandevesky, County Tyrone, had dates in the mid fourth millennium BC for burials in chambers III and I. A few sites with plain Neolithic pottery have dates of *c.*3800–3400 BC, while decorated wares probably belong to the later end of this time span.

Origins and affinities

Irish court tombs should not be viewed in isolation, but as part of a larger group of early to middle Neolithic sites in northern and western Europe. These include portal tombs in Ireland and western Britain, the chambered tombs of the Severn-Cotswold area, the Clyde Cairns of Scotland and 'unchambered' or wooden-chambered long barrows in various regions. The simpler court tombs of east Ulster have a lot in common with the Clyde tombs across the Irish Sea. The full-court and other variant forms of court tomb in the north-west represent a local development in those areas. However, neither the finds nor the radiocarbon dates can be used at present to give a more precise interpretation of the sequence of court-tomb building.

4
Portal tombs

Morphology

The classic definition of a portal tomb was written by de Valera and Ó
Nualláin in Volume I of the *Megalithic Survey of Ireland* (1961) (note
that the term 'portal dolmen' was being used at the time this was written):

> The principal characteristics of portal dolmens are, a single chamber of
> rectilinear design, usually narrowing towards the rear, having an entry
> between two tall portal stones set inside the line of the sidestones and
> covered by a capstone often of enormous size, poised high above the
> entrance and sloping down towards the rear of the chamber. The capstone
> is frequently raised clear of the sidestones and rests on the portal stones
> and backstone. Usually each side and the back are formed of single
> slabs. Frequently beneath the great capstone is a smaller cover resting
> on the sides and backstone and in this case the rear end of the principal
> cap rests on the second cover rather than on the backstone. Between the
> portals a slab closing the entrance is present in many sites, often reaching
> full height, but sometimes only three-quarters or half the height of the
> portal jambs. Occasionally, in place of the high slab a sill is found,
> while in many instances no evidence of closure, partial or full, appears.
> In a few examples high stones flanking the entrance are present. A bias
> towards placing the entrance facing eastwards is present in portal
> dolmens. The mound shape is rarely clearly defined but both long and
> round forms are attested.

While the classic form is widespread (figures 14 and 20), many
variations can be found, such as elongated chambers, as at Brenanstown,
County Dublin (cover photograph), and Poulnabrone, County Clare
(figure 15). Some have the capstone propped on a single orthostat, or on
a small chamber (for example Castle Mary, County Cork, figure 2), and
a few double-chambered tombs are known. A small cist was constructed
within the cairn at Ballykeel, County Armagh (figure 16).

Flanking stones are sometimes found on one or both sides of the
portal stones, forming a simple court. The best-preserved examples are
at Ahaglaslin, County Cork, with a funnel-shaped entrance, while at
Ticloy, County Antrim, there is a crescentic setting of low stones. The
tombs generally face uphill.

Several portal tombs now lack sidestones and look rather like a tripod.
Well-known examples include Legananny, County Down (figure 17),
Proleek, County Louth, and Ballykeel, County Armagh (plan, figure
16). Ballykeel was carefully excavated and no evidence was found of

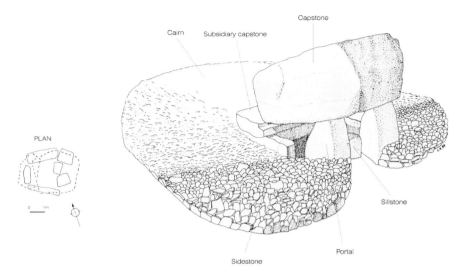

14. Greengraves portal tomb, County Down: reconstruction (after *Archaeological Survey of County Down*).

15. Poulnabrone portal tomb, County Clare. (Photo: author)

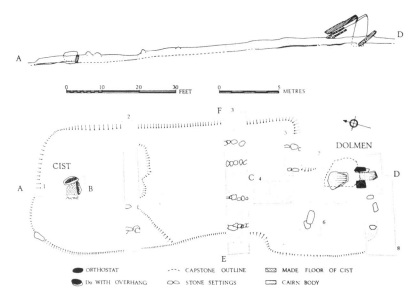

16. Ballykeel portal tomb, County Armagh: excavation plan (after Collins 1965). (By permission of the Department of the Environment, Northern Ireland, and the *Ulster Journal of Archaeology*)

any sockets to hold sidestones although the chamber area was quite well defined by the occurrence of a range of potsherds and other finds. A. E. P. Collins, who excavated the site, concluded that some form of side walling must have been present when the burials and artefacts were placed in the tomb. He suggested three possible types of walling that could have been used: wooden hurdles, dry-stone walling or slabs set in shallow sockets or even propped on the lowest levels of the cairn. The last suggestion is supported by the fact that the backstone was set in a very shallow socket,

17. Legananny portal tomb, County Down: 'tripod' portal tomb. (Photo: author)

18. Arderawinny portal tomb, County Cork. (Photo: L. Snodgrass)

contained in the cairn rather than being cut into the ground. At Aghnaskeagh A, County Louth, similarly, no trace of any type of side walls was found. However, at the 'tripod' site of Pentre Ifan in Wales a dry-stone-wall revetment defined the chamber area.

The capstones can be of extraordinary size, notably at Kernanstown, County Carlow (which weighs nearly 150 tonnes), and Carrickglass, County Sligo. Subsidiary capstones have been noted at sixteen portal tombs – this is where a smaller capstone was placed on the sidestones and backstone so that the lower end of the main capstone rested on the smaller capstone rather than on the orthostats (for example, Knockeen, County Waterford, figure 20). The spaces between the sidestones and the roof may have been closed by corbels, a few of which survive, for example, at Burren, County Cavan. The question has always been asked as to how these stones were set on top of the chambers and, although it can never be proved absolutely, it seems that the most likely method was that a ramp of earth and/or stones was built up to the level of the tops of the orthostats, and the capstones were then hauled up the ramp using ropes and rollers made of tree trunks and pushed into place over the chamber.

No trace of a cairn or mound survives in the majority of portal tombs, and it is now believed that these were never particularly high, merely stabilising the base of the tomb. Long cairns are recorded at about twenty-eight sites, all in the north. Only a few of these have been excavated, notably Ballykeel, County Armagh (figure 16), where several

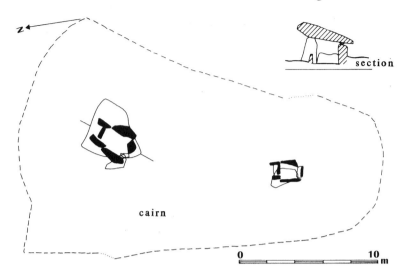

19. Kilclooney More portal tomb, County Donegal. (Courtesy the National Monuments Section, Department of the Environment, Heritage and Local Government)

sections were cut across the cairn, revealing a probable line of dry-built revetment at the edge of the cairn and two lines of stones running along the axis of the cairn. Excavation at Melkagh, County Longford, also revealed traces of a dry-built revetment at the edge of the cairn.

In several sites where more than one chamber occurs, the cairn seems to have had an elongated form, the most spectacular example being at Malin More, County Donegal, where two large portal tombs were built 90 metres apart at each end of a long cairn, with four smaller examples set in line between them. Other multi-chambered sites include Kilclooney More, County Donegal (figure 19), and Ballyrenan, County Tyrone, each with a pair of portal tombs facing in the same direction. However, none of these sites has been excavated and it is possible that they were built in more than one phase. At Dyffryn Ardudwy in Wales, excavation showed that the first phase of construction was a small portal tomb with forecourt set in a more or less circular cairn. Subsequently a cruder tomb was built in front of the first tomb, facing in the same direction, and a long rectangular cairn enveloped both structures. Sub-circular or short oval cairns have also been found in Ireland, for example at Poulnabrone, County Clare (figures 5 and 15), Arderawinny, County Cork (figure 18), and Taylorsgrange, County Dublin.

Distribution and topography

As can be seen from the map (figure 21), the distribution of the 180 portal tombs currently recorded is largely northern, but with thirty-eight sites in the south-east, and a small number in Cork, Clare and Galway. In 1983 Ó Nualláin calculated that 43.5 per cent of the sites are within 8 km of the coast, with many of the inland sites occurring along river valleys. Half the sites are on valley slopes or hillsides and nearly all are placed on terraces or small level tracts of ground, which would be convenient for building. Only nine are on valley floors and the majority (70 per cent) lie below the 120 metre contour.

Burial practices

Excavations at portal tombs have been confined mainly to investigations of the chamber area and most had already been dug out by treasure seekers. The most informative burial deposit investigated was at Poulnabrone, County Clare, where Ann Lynch carried out excavations in 1986 and 1988 in advance of conservation (figures 5 and 15). The burials recovered from the chamber comprised at least sixteen adults and six juveniles. The bones were found in a disarticulated

20. Knockeen portal tomb, County Waterford. (Photo: author)

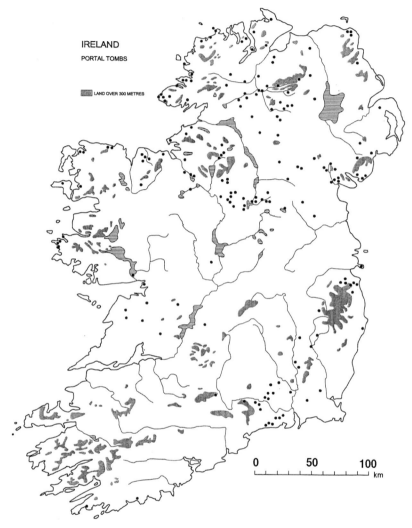

21. Map of Irish portal tombs. (2003: courtesy the National Monuments Section, Department of the Environment, Heritage and Local Government)

condition within the limestone grikes under the tomb chamber, and it is thought that the bodies may have been exposed elsewhere, to allow the flesh to decompose before the bones were collected for deposition in the tomb. Alternatively, they may have been buried elsewhere until the flesh decayed, as they were radiocarbon-dated to *c*.3800–3200 BC.

Only one of the adults lived beyond forty years and the majority were under thirty when they died. A number of artefacts were found with the burials: a polished stone axe, two stone disc beads, a perforated bone pendant, part of a bone pin, two quartz crystals, flint and chert arrowheads and scrapers, and over sixty sherds of pottery of indeterminate form.

In contrast, excavation in 1963 at Ballykeel, County Armagh, by A. E. P. Collins produced a considerable quantity of pottery but only a small amount of flint. The pottery comprised fine plain Neolithic ware, which seems likely to pre-date the tomb's construction as most of it was found outside the chamber area, and three elaborately decorated 'bipartite' bowls (figure 22). Nearly 6 kg of coarse pottery was found, which the excavator believed had been used on the site both before and during construction, and it was also found with the decorated pottery in the funerary deposit.

In all, finds have been reported from less than twenty passage tombs. Apart from Ballykeel, only small quantities of pottery have been found; these include sherds of plain and decorated fine bowls and also coarse ware, some of which is flat-bottomed. Leaf-shaped arrowheads were found at four sites, hollow scrapers at three and well-made scrapers of various types at Ballykeel. There were stone beads at a few sites, and a

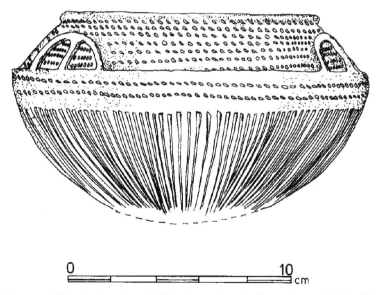

22. Decorated 'bipartite' pot from Ballykeel portal tomb, County Armagh (after Collins 1965). (By permission of the Department of the Environment, Northern Ireland, and the *Ulster Journal of Archaeology*)

small axe of porcellanite from County Antrim was found at Drumanone, County Roscommon.

Apart from Poulnabrone, information on burial rites is also fairly scanty. At Ballykeel no burial remains were found but the high levels of phosphate in the chamber area suggested the former presence of burials that had been destroyed in the highly acidic, granite-derived soil. Cremated bone is reported at eight sites, generally in small quantities, except at Aghnaskeagh (four persons) and at Drumanone, where there were several cremations.

Origins, affinities and dating

The similarities between portal tombs and court tombs have long been recognised in regard to distribution, cairn shape, siting, orientation, grave goods and morphology. The debate is ongoing as to their relationship, several archaeologists arguing that portal tombs developed from court tombs, probably in the mid-Ulster area, mainly because of the similarity between the subsidiary chambers of court tombs in that area and the portal tombs. Others have suggested that portal tombs are earlier than court tombs, which sees support in the apparent conversion of Drumhallagh Upper, County Donegal, from a portal tomb to a court tomb, and Eamon Cody has suggested that 'portal tombs may have taken on some of the features of court tombs such as the long cairn and subsidiary chambers'. The excavation of the central tomb (Number 51, Listoghil) in the passage-tomb cemetery at Carrowmore, County Sligo, has shown that the original monument here may have been a portal tomb, which was later covered over with a large round cairn, and became the focal point for the whole cemetery. Interestingly it appears to be the only one of many tombs excavated in the cemetery to produce inhumations rather than cremations.

The only useful radiocarbon dates from a portal tomb are those from the burials at Poulnabrone, County Clare (*c.*3800–3200 BC), but it is not clear if the tomb was built at the beginning of this period, with deposition of burials over nearly half a millennium, or if the bones were stored elsewhere until the tomb was constructed in the late fourth millennium BC.

Between thirty-five and fifty tombs of the same type have been recorded in Wales and Cornwall, and the siting and general morphology of these is very similar to the Irish sites. Again radiocarbon dates are lacking but the early pottery from Dyffryn Ardudwy suggests a date in the earlier fourth millennium for at least some of the portal tombs in mid Wales.

5
Passage tombs

A passage tomb consists basically of a passage leading to a burial chamber. Of all the tomb groups, this is the one with most variation in size and form, ranging from sites with a simple chamber and short passage to the very elaborate structures such as Newgrange and Knowth in the Boyne valley (*Brú na Bóinne*), County Meath (figure 23). Both of these monuments have been extensively excavated and readers are referred to O'Kelly's 1982 report on Newgrange and Eogan's interim report on Knowth, which was published in 1986.

Design and structure

The *passages* are built with orthostats and roofed by lintels, but their length varies from 1 or 2 metres to over 40 metres at Knowth 1 east (figure 27). The *chambers* likewise vary in size and shape, from a simple round, rectangular or polygonal plan, 1 to 2 metres in diameter, to the exceptionally large chamber at Fourknocks, County

23. Map of sites in the Boyne valley, County Meath. (Based on Ordnance Survey by permission of the Government, permit number 5058)

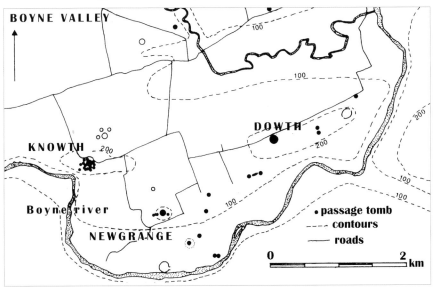

24. Ringarogy, intertidal passage tomb, County Cork. (Photo: author)

Meath (figure 25). One or more recesses open off the chamber at many sites, producing a wide variety of plans. One form has a pair of side chambers with an end chamber, producing a 'cruciform' plan (figure 26). In other sites a large main chamber was subdivided by orthostats into a series of small cells or chambers (Loughcrew, County Meath,

25. Fourknocks passage tomb, County Meath. (Photo: Department of the Environment, Heritage and Local Government)

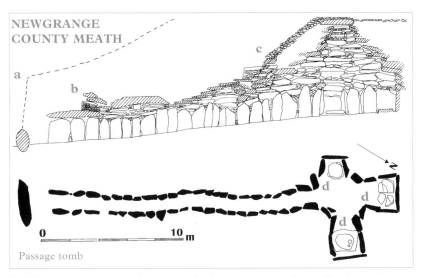

26. Newgrange passage tomb, County Meath: a, suggested cairn profile; b, roof box; c, 'mini-cairn'; d, chambers/cells (after O'Kelly 1982). (By permission of Mrs C. O'Kelly)

Cairns I and L, figure 4). Low *sill stones* are usually set at the entrances to the recesses and sometimes across the junction of the passage and chamber or across the passage. Most of the best-known sites have a cruciform plan but sites with simple polygonal chambers or with little differentiation between passage and chamber are actually more numerous (for example, Ringarogy, County Cork, figure 24, and several of the smaller Knowth sites, figure 27). In the simple tombs, a single capstone usually covers the chamber (for example Carrowmore 7, County Sligo, figure 28). The chamber at Fourknocks (diameter 5.5–6.4 metres, figure 25) was probably covered by some form of wooden roof supported on a wooden post, which was set in a posthole that was found roughly in the centre of the chamber. A corbelled roof survives at the two largest cruciform sites, reaching a height of 6 metres at Newgrange (figure 26) and 5.9 metres at Knowth 1 east (figure 29). The excavations at Newgrange showed that the corbelled roof was built as a free-standing structure with its own 'mini-cairn', the outside of which was held in place by a built revetment of boulders (figure 26c). This mini-cairn provided a counterweight on the tails of the roof corbels, to prevent them from tumbling into the chamber. Another feature of the roof at Newgrange was the discovery of grooves or water channels cut on the upper surfaces of the passage lintels. These were up to 5 cm wide and 1 cm deep and were designed to drain rainwater outwards on to each side of the passage, thus keeping the tomb completely dry, even to this day.

Cairns covering passage tombs are basically circular in plan, though many sites have a flattening or inturning of the cairn edge in front of the tomb entrance. A line of kerbstones usually delimits the edge of the cairn, though some have a dry-stone wall edging. At Newgrange, excavation indicated that a dry-stone wall had been built on top of the kerbstones as a revetment to the cairn material. It was estimated that the wall sloped inwards at an angle of about 40 degrees, and that it was originally about 3 metres high, but apparently it collapsed outwards quite soon after it was built. The front (south-east) façade was built with both white quartz (possibly from the Wicklow Mountains) and grey/ black granites (almost certainly collected around Dundalk Bay, 30 km up the coast) whereas round the sides and the back of the monument the walling was built from the same local stone as was used in the cairn. Quartz has been found near the entrances of other passage tombs and was obviously significant – it continues to be used on graves up to the present time. Dry-built walls have been found on top of kerbstones at several passage tombs, particularly in County Sligo, and also at Baltinglass and Loughcrew. The term 'cairn' is generally taken to indicate a mainly stone composition, but excavations at several passage tombs have shown that many contain a considerable amount of earth or turves, usually in layers between the stones. At several sites, rings of low stones have been found on the old ground surface inside the kerb.

Evidence of settlement has been found beneath the mounds of several passage tombs, most notably at Knowth, where remains have been found of at least five rectangular plank-built houses constructed after 4000 BC. Soon afterwards other structures, including a double-palisade enclosure, were built, followed by at least nine circular houses associated with decorated pottery (c.3500–3300 BC), including Carrowkeel ware (see below), which appear to be contemporary with the passage tomb.

Orientation

Passage tombs vary considerably in their orientation, with examples facing to all points of the compass. There is a slight preference for east-south-east, but many sites appear to be focused on another group of monuments or a significant site in the landscape. At both Knowth (figure 27) and Carrowmore, County Sligo, the tombs mostly face towards a central space or feature. The four Newgrange tombs face between south-east and south-west, towards the river. The Carrowkeel/Keshcorran group in County Sligo face north-westwards, towards the monuments on the Cúil Irra peninsula. The passage tombs at Loughcrew can be seen from inside the passage tomb on Slieve Gullion, 60 km to the north.

Some very specific orientations have been noted, with the sun shining into several tombs at the solstices and equinoxes. The best-known

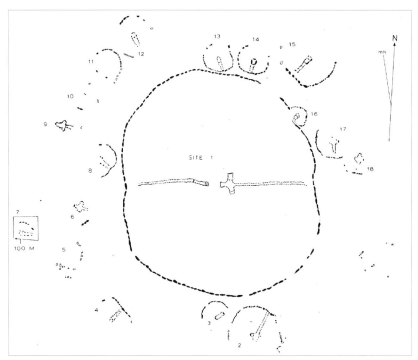

27. Knowth passage tombs, County Meath (after Eogan 1986). (By permission of Professor G. Eogan and Ms H. Richardson)

example is at Newgrange, where what has been called a 'roof box' was built 2.3 metres back from the start of the passage (figure 26, b). The roof box was constructed of a horizontal slab that was supported on low walls and positioned over a gap between two of the passage lintels, thus forming a slot. It has been found that the rising sun on midwinter's day shines through the slot in the roof box and a beam of sunlight projects along the passage, across the chamber, and reaches right into the end chamber. This phenomenon occurs for a week or so before and after 21st December, but only on the day of the winter solstice itself does the beam of light reach the end chamber. At Dowth, 2 km east of Newgrange (figure 23), the setting sun shines into the smaller of the two tombs on midwinter's day. Midwinter's day was also marked at Knockroe, County Kilkenny, where the two tombs in the cairn are orientated on the setting and the rising sun on that day. Equinoxes are captured at the two tombs at Knowth, and also at Cairn T, the highest of the Loughcrew group of tombs, where the early sunlight illuminates a series of radial line patterns that are carved on stones along the axis of the tomb.

Distribution and topography

The distribution of the 236 known passage tombs is mainly northern and eastern, with 63 per cent of all monuments concentrated within a 30 km wide band running from the mouth of the river Boyne to Sligo. Many large cairns sited on hilltops elsewhere in Ireland would need excavation or geophysical techniques to check for the presence of a megalithic chamber, since hilltop cairns were also constructed in the Bronze Age to contain small cist burials. It has been suggested that a number of cairns on prominent hilltops in the south-west may conceal passage tombs – a definite example is known at Killickaforavane, Clear Island, County Cork, while a rather unusual version of a passage tomb has been excavated at Ballycarty, County Kerry.

Passage tombs were often built in groups or 'cemeteries', with cluster sizes varying from three or four tombs to the large group of about sixty sites at Carrowmore, County Sligo. Nearly forty sites extend over 16 square km in the Boyne valley (figure 23), with clusters of twenty sites at Knowth and four (or five) sites at Newgrange. Loughcrew (*Sliabh na Caillighe*) has about twenty-five monuments and Carrowkeel/Keshcorran has about twenty. The biggest tomb of a group may be on the highest point of its ridge, as at both Newgrange and Knocknarea, County Sligo (figure 28), where one or two smaller tombs form a row on each side of the main cairn. However, on the western hill at Loughcrew the smaller tombs occupy individual knolls, while the biggest cairn (D) is built in a saddle on the hill. At Carrowmore, the largest tomb, Number 51 (Listoghil), is on comparatively flat ground, though this may be because this is actually a portal tomb that later became a focus for a passage-tomb cemetery and was

28. Carrowmore (Tomb 7) and Knocknarea, County Sligo. (Photo: author)

29. Knowth,
County Meath:
corbelled roof.
(Photo:
Department of
the
Environment,
Heritage and
Local
Government)

covered over with a very large cairn. Some sites are positioned
conspicuously, so that from the lowlands they have the appearance of
being on the highest point. Over half of all passage tombs are below the
150 metre contour, and a small tomb has been recorded in the estuary of
the Ilen River, near Baltimore, County Cork (figure 24).

Burial practices

Hartnett's work at Fourknocks in the early 1950s marked the start of a
phase of extensive excavations at Irish passage tombs and work began
at both Newgrange and Knowth in 1962. O'Kelly's fourteen seasons of
investigations at Newgrange were published in 1982 and Eogan has
published several interim reports on Knowth. The first campaigns of
excavations by Burenhult at Carrowmore have also been published but
interesting excavations such as Tara and Knockroe are currently known
only from interim reports.

Cremated remains have been found at nearly all excavated sites, with
occasional occurrences of unburnt bones, particularly skull fragments
and children's bones. Burials are most usually found in the tomb
chamber, but at some sites they have been found outside the tomb (for
example at Tara). In the chambers, burials seem to have been placed
directly on the old ground surface or on flagstones or basin stones.
There is some evidence for sealing over of burial deposits once they
were placed in the tomb. Burials were also inserted in the passage at
Fourknocks, though this may well have been done after the main phase
of burials. Individual deposits of cremated bone have been reported in

Knowth 1 east, with at least six deposits of cremated bone in the east recess, each covered by a thin layer of earth or small flat stones. The number of individuals buried at each site varies – only one was found at each of four small tombs at Knowth, but high numbers have been reported at Tara and Fourknocks. At Newgrange the only remains found were two unburnt burials and about three cremations, but here the small numbers are surely explained by the fact that the site has been open for nearly three hundred years. A possible crematorium was excavated at Fourknocks II, near the passage tomb, where a stone-built passage led to the middle of a long trench, in which fires had been lit, and deposits of earth, charcoal and cremated bone may have resulted from cremation *in situ*.

The chambers of many of the more elaborate passage tombs have a *basin stone*, generally consisting of a large, hollowed-out slab or block of stone. About twenty examples are known, and some sites have more than one basin. They are usually found in the side or end chambers and occupy most of the space inside these chambers. One basin from Newgrange and an elaborately carved one from Knowth are of granite from the Mourne Mountains. The role of the basin seems to have been as a container for cremations, though at most sites the remains have been found displaced from the basin on to the ground surface around it.

A wide variety of *artefacts* has been found accompanying the burial deposits in most passage tombs (figure 33) and, unlike those from the other tomb types, these seem to be special pieces that would not have been used on a day-to-day basis. Pottery of a type called 'Carrowkeel ware' is found almost exclusively at passage tombs. The bowls have a distinctive ornament jabbed on to the clay with a pointed implement. A range of pendants and beads has been found, which may be made from bone, baked clay or from a variety of rare stone types such as jasper, carnelian or serpentine. Balls averaging 10–20 mm in diameter have also been found in many tombs. Most are of chalk but baked clay, bone and stone examples are also known. A conjoined pair was found at Newgrange. Pins of bone or antler are commonly found and a few are decorated with incised chevron designs (figure 33, 12). Some have a bulbous expansion at the top and are referred to as 'mushroom' or 'poppy' headed (figure 33, 6–7). Some stone axes, flint and chert scrapers and projectile points are also known from passage tombs. A most unusual object was found near the entrance to the western tomb at Knowth; this was an elaborately polished and carved pointed stone about 250 mm long, possibly representing a phallus; another, but without decoration, was found near the entrance to Newgrange. Similar objects are known from tombs in southern Portugal. A small but magnificently worked flint macehead was found in the chamber at Knowth 1 east (figure 34);

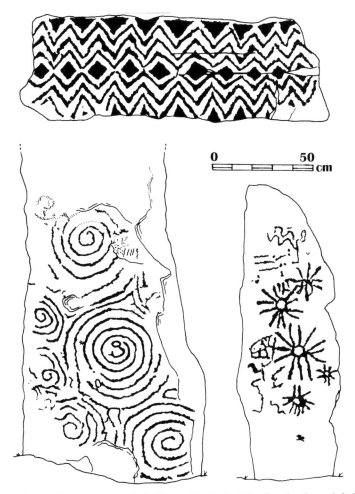

30. Carved stones from passage tombs in County Meath: (top) Fourknocks; (lower left) King's Mountain; (lower right) Loughcrew Cairn I (after Shee Twohig, *The Megalithic Art of Western Europe*, Oxford University Press, 1981). (By permission of the Clarendon Press, Oxford)

it is decorated with spiral designs on four surfaces and a network of lozenges at each end. Originally it would have been mounted on a shaft and would have functioned as some form of emblem. However, the form of this piece, and the designs on it, are not typically associated with passage tombs, and it was probably placed in the tomb in the later Neolithic period. Part of an undecorated macehead was found in the western tomb.

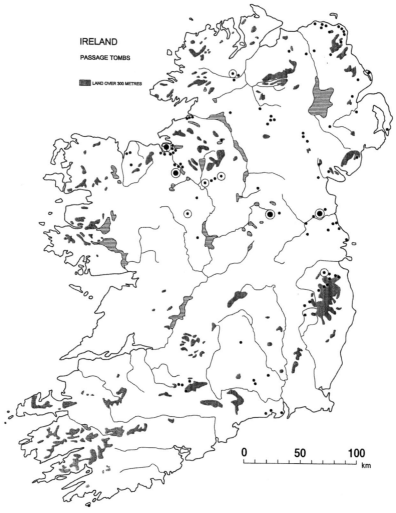

31. Map of Irish passage tombs. A small dot indicates 1–2 sites; a small dot in a circle denotes 3–8 sites, and a large dot in a circle 9 or more sites. (2003: courtesy the National Monuments Section, Heritage and Planning Division, Department of the Environment, Heritage and Local Government)

Excavations also revealed a number of ritual features outside the tomb entrances at the Boyne valley passage tombs; these included standing stones, arcs and oval settings of stones. Oval settings were found in front of both the tomb entrances at Knowth 1 and at Newgrange, with a central paved area edged by carefully placed small stones, many

32. Newgrange, County Meath: aerial view from the north, showing excavations in progress at the back of the cairn in 1988. The river Boyne is visible in the background and the small passage tombs K, L and Z are marked. (Photo: D. L. Swan)

of which had been brought from around Dundalk Bay about 30 km north along the coast from the river mouth. A similar feature is reported from outside Loughcrew Cairn T. The foundations of an oval hut were also uncovered near the setting at Newgrange.

Carvings

A distinctive feature of passage tombs is the occurrence of carved designs on many of the tomb orthostats and roof stones (figure 30). This is found in various tombs in the eastern part of Ireland, from Antrim to south Kilkenny, with a single stone recorded from Cape Clear Island, County Cork (though this is not definitely from a passage tomb). A single example of carving has been recorded in the north-west, at the central tomb at Carrowmore 51 (Listoghil). As already suggested, this may originally have been a portal tomb, with the carvings (on the front edge of the capstone) perhaps added at the time of its conversion to a passage tomb.

Well-preserved carvings show that the lines were made with a series of pick marks, and experiments have shown that a sharply pointed implement of flint or quartzite could have produced such marks when tapped home with a mallet or hammerstone. Alternatively, they could have been done by direct percussion, using some sort of hammerstone. Incised or scratched designs are also known, sometimes used to outline or 'rough out' a design for later completion by picking, but also on occasions as a technique in its own right. No traces of paint have been found in any Irish tomb, though in the drier climate of western Iberia red and black painting on a white background has been found in contemporary passage tombs. The motifs used in Irish passage tombs have so far defied interpretation. For the most part they are geometric in form, comprising circles, spirals, lozenges, zigzags, triangles, et cetera (figure 30). Occasionally a particular juxtaposition of motifs may give the appearance of a face or torso, but these are very rare and may be quite illusory, and no identifiable objects are represented. While it is disappointing not to be able to understand the meaning behind these carvings, one cannot but marvel at the artistic quality of some of the carved stones and the elegant simplicity of others. Several compositions are very impressive, such as the famous entrance stone at Newgrange, and the basin stone in Knowth, while the angular carvings at Fourknocks have a sort of architectural quality (figure 30, top). A wide range of styles can be identified at Knowth, where many carvers must have worked at different times. Over three hundred carved stones have now been recorded at Knowth, which is by far the largest number known at any site in western Europe.

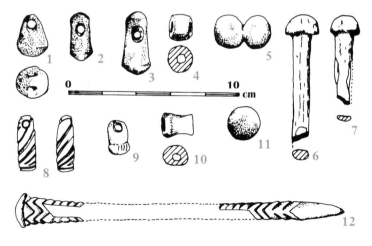

33. Artefacts from passage tombs in County Meath: 1-2, 5 and 11, Newgrange (after O'Kelly 1982); 3, 4, 10 and 12, Fourknocks (after Hartnett 1956); 6-7 Loughcrew R (after Herity); 8-9 Tara (after Herity). (Numbers 1, 2, 5 and 11 by permission of Mrs C. O'Kelly; numbers 6-9 by permission of Professor M. Herity)

34. Decorated macehead from Knowth, County Meath; drawing 'unfolded' to show the four decorated surfaces. Maximum length of macehead 79 mm (after Eogan and Richardson, 1982). (By permission of Professor G. Eogan and Ms H. Richardson)

Dating

Newgrange and the main mound at Knowth have a series of radiocarbon dates that place them in the later part of the fourth millennium BC (*c*.3500–3000 BC). Other than these, almost no reliably dated samples are published, but it seems reasonable to envisage the development of a local tradition of passage-tomb building in Ireland before the erection of the major Boyne valley tombs. The overall picture of passage-tomb building seems likely to suggest a beginning by (at least) the middle of the fourth millennium and continuation right through until the early third millennium, while a general development from simple to complex sites seems to be the most likely scenario. A large number of dates have been published from the excavations at Carrowmore, but the contexts of most of the samples are not clearly explained in the publications of the work done in the 1980s. Full publication of the more recent dates may help clarify the sequence of events there.

Later activities around passage tombs

Passage tombs and their surroundings continued to be important for succeeding generations, and large ritual earthworks and timber settings or structures were built in the Boyne valley in the later third millennium and beyond (precise dates are again lacking). At Newgrange one large timber structure (about 100 metres in diameter) and one small one (about 20 metres in diameter) were built, while at Knowth a small but very substantial timber building was placed in front of the entrance to the eastern tomb. A range of artefacts was deposited at these sites and, at Knowth, pottery and Antrim flints were placed adjacent to the posts when the postholes were backfilled. The circle of standing stones at Newgrange was also built around this time. In the wider valley area are several large earthwork enclosures, known as henge monuments, one of which (Monknewtown) has proved on excavation to be broadly contemporary with the timber circles. More examples of associations between passage tombs and timber circles and/or enclosures are known elsewhere in County Meath, at Fourknocks and Tara, and also at Ballynahatty, County Down. These monuments see a change in the style of pottery, with people using a flat-bottomed ware called 'Grooved ware', followed by the introduction of 'Beaker' pottery, with its highly decorated drinking vessels, which is found throughout western Europe.

Outside the Boyne valley, people frequently placed burials into the chamber or the cairn of passage tombs in the earlier Bronze Age (*c.*2300– 1800 BC) together with small vases or bowls known as food vessels. At a slightly later date, larger pots (urns) containing cremated remains were sometimes placed in the megalithic tombs. On the threshold of history, Newgrange was the scene of ritual activities involving the deposition of valuable gold coins and ornaments from Roman Britain while some Roman material was also found at Knowth.

Origins and affinities

The Irish passage tombs are part of a widespread distribution of monuments of this type, built in many regions of western Europe, in the areas that are now Spain and Portugal, Denmark and southern Sweden, southern and western France, and western and northern Britain. In most areas the dating evidence suggests that the simple polygonal passage tomb is the earliest form, appearing *c.*4500 BC or before in the western Mediterranean zone, with the more elaborate sites developing during the fourth millennium. Some elements of the Irish sites can be found elsewhere, notably carvings, which occur in various parts of Spain and Portugal, in Brittany, and in a few British sites, and it seems likely that there was some connection between these areas. However, there is not much similarity between the artefacts that accompany the burials in the various regions, except for the distinctive phallic cylinders from Knowth and Newgrange, which have close parallels in southern Portugal.

6
Wedge tombs

Wedge tombs consist of a main chamber or gallery, which generally lies on a north-east to south-west axis. Many tombs have a small portico or antechamber at the western end and some have a small chamber at the eastern end (figure 36). The tombs are generally wider and higher at the western end (figures 38 and 41) and are thus 'wedge-shaped' in both plan and profile. Tomb lengths vary between 2 metres and 10–11 metres, with most of the larger monuments in the north of the country, though some large examples occur also in north Munster, for example at Labbacallee, County Cork (figure 41).

Design and structure

At most sites the sides of the tomb consist of a number of orthostats set in line. A second row of stones was generally set up outside the gallery, at 1–2 metres from the tomb walls, where it probably delimited

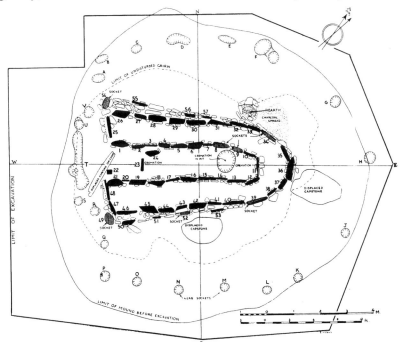

35. Island wedge tomb, County Cork: excavation plan (after O'Kelly 1958). (By permission of Mrs C. O'Kelly)

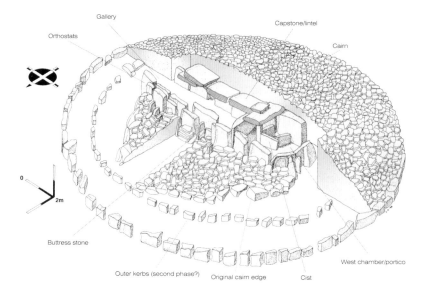

36. Baurnadomeeny wedge tomb, County Tipperary: reconstruction drawing (after O'Kelly 1958).

37. Ballynahown wedge tomb, County Clare, situated in the characteristic limestone landscape of the Burren. (Photo: Megalithic Survey; by permission of the Department of the Environment, Heritage and Local Government)

the edge of the cairn (for example, Boviel, County Derry, figure 42). Sometimes, however, the second row was set contiguous with the tomb wall, and three rows of orthostats were set close together at Labbacallee, County Cork (figure 41). In some areas where large slabs were available, only one or two stones were used for the tomb sides and roof; this is particularly noticeable in the limestone of the Burren in County Clare, where the readily available slabs were used to build large, 2–3 metres long wedge-shaped boxes (figure 37). Small stones were sometimes set at right angles outside the tomb walls, as if to buttress the orthostats (figure 36).

The western chamber ('portico') could be separated from the main chamber in a variety of ways: by jambs, by a tall septal slab, by a sill stone, or by two door slabs. Free-standing pillar stones of varying heights were sometimes set up in the portico, perhaps as a roof support. The form of segmentation was probably related to the practices at the monuments, and certain regional preferences have been identified, for example the occurrence of the double door in the Burren. The western chambers seem to have remained accessible, but if there was a septal slab one could not get from them into the main chamber. This type of segmentation is common in west Tipperary and east Clare (figure 36).

The eastern end of the tomb was usually closed with a single slab, but some sites have a small chamber at this end of the main chamber. Some sites have no evidence of closure at the eastern end, though this may have been effected with a movable stone slab or a flimsy one that has disappeared with time.

38. Altar wedge tomb, County Cork, viewed from the west (front) end of the tomb. (Photo: author)

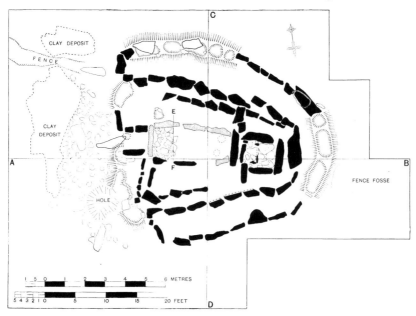

39. Ballyedmonduff wedge tomb, County Dublin: excavation plan (after Ó Riordáin and de Valera 1952). (By permission of the Royal Irish Academy)

Wedge tombs were roofed with lintels/capstones, which were generally placed directly on the orthostats, though some pad stones have been noted, and there are a few examples of corbelling. Some of the western chambers may not have been roofed and may have functioned as a type of forecourt (for example, at Ballybriest, County Derry).

Wedge tombs generally had a U-shaped cairn, edged by the outer line of orthostats/kerbstones (figures 35, 39 and 42). As is so common with megalithic tombs generally, the stones have often been robbed from the cairn, making it difficult to determine the original plan during field survey. A straight façade of orthostats was often built along the front of the tomb (figures 35 and 39), with the highest stones of the façade nearest the tomb entrance. Revetments of orthostats or low boulders are sometimes found within the cairn (for example, Ballyedmonduff, County Dublin, figure 39) and these may mark the original edge of the cairn. Full excavation of the area around the monument at Island (figure 35) revealed a series of kerbstone sockets, which were set so far apart that the excavator suggested that they were linked by stretches of dry-stone walling to delimit the cairn edge. Similar sockets set in an arc in front of the tomb entrance were interpreted as having held the base of further cairn stones that would have blocked off the tomb once it had gone out of use. However, radiocarbon dates from this site suggest the possibility that the outer setting was added to the monument in the middle Bronze Age. The rare occurrence of round cairns may also be a secondary feature, to cover Bronze Age burials, as seems likely at Baurnadomeeny (figure 36).

'Cupmarks' or circular hollows averaging 5 cm in diameter have been recorded on the capstones of many wedge tombs or on orthostats or small stone slabs associated with the monuments, and these must have had some symbolism for the builders. Examples are reported at a number of County Derry sites and at Baurnadomeeny and Ballyedmonduff. Incised markings on the inner face of the portico orthostat at Baurnadomeeny seem likely to be an original feature because they terminate exactly along the line of the old ground level. Similar markings at other tombs are difficult to date and might be quite recent.

Distribution and topography

A total of 543 wedge tombs were on record in 2003 (figure 40). The distribution is markedly western, with high densities in Munster, particularly in Clare and in mid Cork and the coastal area of Kerry and west Cork. Only about thirteen sites are recorded in the eastern part of Ireland. Given the rare occurrence of other tomb forms in most of Munster, the wedge tombs were essentially the first tombs built in most of this region. In the Dingle peninsula, County Kerry, field survey has identified several examples of wedge tombs associated with field walls, enclosures, standing stones, carved rock outcrops and cooking places (for example around Lough Adoon). However, only excavation could determine if these monuments were all in use at the same time.

Wedge tombs were built over a wide range of altitudes, with a comparatively large number of them on high ground, perhaps indicating an extension of settlement on to the uplands at the end of the Neolithic period.

Burial practices

About twenty-eight wedge tombs have been excavated, and there are chance finds from several more sites. However, owing to disturbance at many sites, it is not always possible to distinguish original burials and accompanying artefacts from later additions. The sites in the northern part of the country have generally produced more material, and very little has been found at the seven sites excavated in south Munster.

Human remains were found at most of the excavated sites. As with other tomb types, cremation was the preferred option, though some inhumations are also recorded. Radiocarbon dates have been obtained

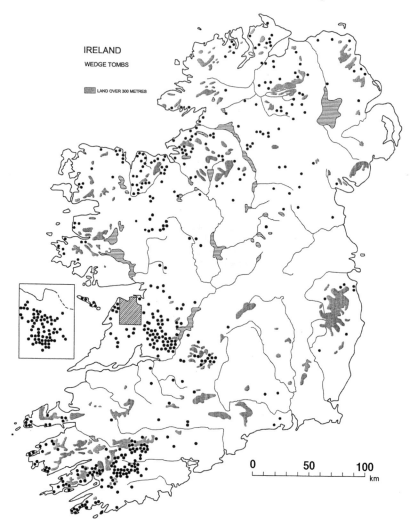

40. Map of Irish wedge tombs. (2003: courtesy the National Monuments Section, Department of the Environment, Heritage and Local Government)

from samples of human bone from a number of sites (see below under 'Dating'). At Ballybriest, County Derry, a number of deposits of cremated bone were found, the largest of which, in the main chamber, contained at least seven individuals, including an adult male, a female, a child of two to five years and an infant. At Baurnadomeeny, County Tipperary (figure 36), the main chamber had been dug out in antiquity but a number of cremations were identified; one was in a small cist in the portico while several found outside the tomb probably belonged to a phase of enlargement of the cairn in the Bronze Age. Nine individuals (five adults and four juveniles) were identified from one section of an otherwise very disturbed deposit of inhumation burials at Lough Gur. At Island, County Cork, three primary cremations were found, one of which was a female aged sixty to seventy years. Two sites, Altar (figure 38) and Toormore on the Mizen peninsula of west Cork, meticulously excavated by William O'Brien, were shown to have been used over a long period of time. At Altar the earliest deposit consisted of a cremation accompanied by an unburnt human tooth. At Toormore the suggested period for tomb construction is also *c*.2000–1750 BC, and this fits well with the typology of a bronze axehead which was placed in the tomb entrance together with two pieces of raw copper.

Beaker pottery has now been found at about ten sites, mainly in the north-west. This term refers to a type of pottery that is found widely throughout Europe, dating from around 2500 BC onwards, and is generally taller than Neolithic pots. Many Beakers are quite thin-walled and finely decorated, and it is thought that they were used as prestige drinking vessels, perhaps for an alcoholic drink. Owing to disturbance

41. Labbacallee wedge tomb, County Cork. (Photo: author)

at many sites it has not been possible to be certain that the Beaker pottery found at wedge tombs definitely belonged to the builders of the tomb. However, at least six Beakers were found at Ballybriest, County Derry, most of which appear to be contemporary with the original period of use of the monument. One of these pots is reputed to be the biggest Beaker recorded in western Europe, being 50 cm high and having a capacity of about 9.5 litres! In contrast, a Beaker from Largantea in north County Derry is only 8 cm high. Generally only a few undiagnostic flint tools have been found at wedge tombs, but examples of barbed and tanged arrowheads are recorded at several sites, of a form that is often found with Beaker ceramics in Britain and continental Europe.

In the past, Neolithic pottery has been claimed at several sites, but most of this pottery is quite undiagnostic and could just as easily belong to the Bronze Age. At Lough Gur there was considerable disturbance, and the Neolithic pottery was probably on site before the tomb was constructed. At Boviel, County Derry (figure 42), Neolithic pottery was found, together with stone axes and Neolithic flint artefacts. The excavators' records suggest that this material belonged to the primary use of the tomb, but here again the tomb was very disturbed. Many wedge tombs continued to be used for burial throughout the earlier Bronze Age, as is evidenced by funerary pottery such as late Beakers, food-vessel bowls and vases, and urns, some of which were placed in

42. Boviel wedge tomb, County Derry, viewed from the east (rear) of the tomb. (Photo: author)

cists built into the cairn (for example at Kilmashogue, County Dublin) or within the tomb. At Lough Gur, County Limerick, radiocarbon dating of the nine inhumation burials showed one child's burial to be three to four hundred years more recent than the other eight burials dated. Both Altar and Toormore have later deposits – at Altar in the later Bronze Age, while marine shells were deposited in the Iron Age and there is also evidence of early historic and early medieval activity. At Toormore, sediment spreads show activity at the site in the mid to later Bronze Age and in the early Iron Age.

Dating

Radiocarbon dating of human remains and well-contexted charcoal from a number of wedge tombs shows that these sites must now be accepted as being considerably later in date than the other types of megalithic tombs. The dates from human remains at Lough Gur and Labbacallee show that these tombs were used from *c.*2500/2300 BC onwards. Two of the burial deposits at Ballybriest were dated to *c.*2150–1750 BC and the construction of Altar and Toormore is dated to the centuries immediately after 2000 BC. While there still must be some unease about the security of the contexts of the Beaker pottery from most tombs, when taken with the radiocarbon dates it seems likely that the Beaker pottery and barbed and tanged arrowheads are primary at most sites.

Origins and affinities

Many archaeologists have argued that the Irish wedge tombs are derived from or influenced by the late Neolithic gallery graves of Brittany, in north-west France, which are known as *allées couvertes.* These sites are similar in some aspects to the Irish wedge tombs but they are generally much larger than the Irish sites, are entered from the eastern end and do not have the wedge-shaped plan and profile of the Irish tombs. The Irish sites that most resemble the Breton ones are those in west Tipperary, east Limerick and the east Clare highlands, and a movement into those regions via the Shannon estuary might be suggested, with a subsequent two-directional spread, introducing wedge tombs to the south-west and to the north. On the other hand, the tombs may have developed in Ireland. As yet, the dating is not sufficiently precise to determine if any particular group is earlier than another group, but the larger dimensions of the northern tombs and the reflections of court-tomb elements in the flat façade and U-shaped cairns in that area suggest a possible derivation from court tombs in the north.

7
Conclusions

We have seen in the preceding chapters that megalithic tombs began to be built in Ireland in the early fourth millennium BC, initially with court tombs, and possibly portal tombs, but many more secure dates are needed to clarify the situation. The simple passage tombs may also have developed at about this time, with the big sites in the Boyne valley being built towards the end of the fourth millennium. The wedge tombs can now be accepted as being much later in date. We have seen something of the range of activities that took place at these sites, the various burial practices and the artefacts that were put in the tombs with the dead. It is also interesting to note the extent to which these sites continued to play a role in people's lives for later generations, even until the present day, when these sites are seen as an intrinsic part of the Irish heritage.

It is now appropriate to turn to the more difficult questions 'Why were these monuments built?' and 'What type of society was prepared to expend so much time and effort on building houses for the dead?' On the basis of the information from excavations, we can offer some suggestions but, because our data consist of the barest bones and stones, these can never claim to be definitive answers.

Firstly, we need to consider the role of these monuments – should they be regarded as tombs? The answer to this is both 'yes' and 'no'. 'Yes', because people were obviously buried in them, but also 'no', because they clearly functioned as more than just burial places. Let us examine this question under the headings of burials, structure and size, orientation, carvings, artefacts and ceremonial activity.

Burials. Careful consideration shows that the monuments cannot have been built solely or even primarily for burial. Many had very few burials in them and, while in some instances the absence of remains may be due to tomb robbing (for example at Newgrange) or to poor conditions for preservation of bone, the overall impression is that only a very small proportion of the population can have been buried in the monuments. Even taking into account that many sites must have been destroyed over time, a total of sixteen hundred sites built over nearly two thousand years represents the building of less than one monument on the island per year! The actual burials also show evidence of ritual practices, and modern excavations and the post-excavation analysis are able to give us more insights, showing for instance the defleshing of the inhumations at Poulnabrone, while radiocarbon dating proves that these particular burials covered a considerable time span.

Structure and size. The elaborate structure of many tombs, notably the passage tombs and court tombs, argues for their having fulfilled some special role in society. Sites such as Newgrange and Knowth demonstrate a very considerable investment of time and other resources. George Eogan estimated that about two thousand large stones were needed for the orthostats, roof stones and kerbstones used to build the passage tombs in the Boyne valley, apart from the smaller stones used in the cairn construction. Many of these stones were brought from some distance away. The transport of all these materials must have been a major undertaking, even supposing that cattle may have been used for traction, or that the stones may have been brought along the coastline and up river on rafts. O'Kelly calculated that 200,000 tonnes of small stones were used in building the Newgrange mound, and quartz and granite were brought from well outside the area to face the cairns. In addition, many hectares of pasture-land were stripped to provide the layers of sods in the mounds.

Orientation. We have seen that many passage tombs were deliberately orientated on sunrise or sunset at particular times of the year, and this must have required considerable skill to design. Other tomb types may have had specific orientations also, but this has not been investigated to any extent. It is noteworthy, however, that the broadly eastern orientation of court tombs and many portal tombs was changed to a south-western orientation for the wedge tombs.

Carvings. The carvings on the passage tombs provide further evidence of rituals in the tombs; they are clearly not purely decorative but held some symbolic significance for those who executed them and those who saw them.

Artefacts. The deposition of artefacts in the tombs hints at ceremonies and practices about which we can only speculate. Clearly, certain materials were deemed appropriate for deposition, and many of the artefacts (from the passage tombs in particular) are obviously special, and not for everyday use, as they do not occur at settlement sites.

It is clear from the above that the tombs were not built solely for burial and that considerable ritual was involved in their construction and use. We can only guess at the choreography of the ceremonies, but the architecture determines that access to the inner parts of the monuments must have been restricted to certain people, and it is likely that the interpretation of the carvings was also circumscribed, and revealed only to the initiated.

At the start of this book it was noted that megalithic tombs appear in many areas of western Europe at approximately the same stage in the development of society, that is, just when agriculture was introduced. Was there a need for symbols of stability in these changing times? Did the monuments constitute a focal point for a group or tribe, establishing their claim to a territory or marking special places in some way? The scale and conspicuous siting of the cairns, particularly of the passage tombs, suggest that there was a need to impress observers, be they outsiders in search of new territories, or members of the tribe or band who had to be reminded of the necessity for group solidarity and/or the power of the leaders. Other archaeologists see the tombs as important mainly as containers for the bones of the ancestors, and the practice of defleshing bones, and possibly storing them before their final deposition in a megalithic tomb, points towards the significance of the bones in their own right. What were the implications of cremation as opposed to inhumation? Were the artefacts deposited for the use of the dead in the afterlife, or were they tokens offered by the community to signify the kinship and alliances of the deceased or their role in society? Much remains to be investigated, and we can never have definitive answers, but whatever the reasons behind the construction of these monuments, even in their present denuded and often neglected condition, they still hold resonances and connotations at various levels, engendering a response in all but the most cynical observer more than five millennia after their construction.

8
Glossary

Artefact: manufactured object.

Beaker: pottery with distinctive fabric and form, which appears in Ireland *c.*2500/2400 BC, probably as containers for drink.

Bronze Age: period when bronze was first used, and before iron, *c.*2500/2300–800/500 BC.

Cairn: mound of stones, covering a tomb structure.

Cist: small box-like structure in which burials were placed in the Bronze Age.

Coarse ware: pottery with a coarse texture and usually thick-walled. May be Neolithic or Bronze Age.

Corbel: roof stone set at an angle on the orthostats. Further corbels were placed above and cantilevered beyond the previous one to complete the roof.

Dry walling: stone wall or revetment built without mortar.

Grave goods: pottery and other artefacts placed with the dead in a tomb.

Iron Age: period when iron was introduced, *c.*800/500 BC to 500 AD.

Jamb stones: upright stone on each side of a tomb entrance, or segmenting a tomb.

Kerb: stones delimiting the edge of a cairn.

Lintel: horizontal roof slab.

Megalithic: built from large stones, from the Greek *megas* (large) and *lithos* (stone).

Millennium: one thousand years. The fourth millennium BC runs from 4000 to 3000 BC, the third from 3000 to 2000 and so on.

Neolithic: New Stone Age. In Ireland this was the period *c.*4000 BC to 2500/2300 BC, when farming practices developed.

Orthostat: vertical stone.

Portals: tall upright stones on each side of a tomb entrance, particularly in portal tombs.

Radiocarbon dating: scientific method of dating organic material in a laboratory to determine its age at death. Used mainly on charcoal and bone.

Revetment: edging of a cairn or internal support within a cairn, built in dry-stone walling.

9
Sites to visit

The following is a selection of sites to visit, together with details of tomb type, national grid reference and published reference. (An asterisk is used in a grid reference where a number of sites extend beyond a single Ordnance Survey coordinate point.) This is not an exhaustive list and visitors are directed to the guidebooks by Harbison and Hamlin (see Chapter 10) for more information. References given here in short form, e.g. Bergh (1995), will be found in full in Chapter 10, 'Further Reading'. The *Megalithic Survey* (*MS*) volumes contain detailed information on the tombs in several counties and short descriptions are also contained in the *Archaeological Inventories* and *Surveys* for individual counties. Summaries of recent excavations are published in *Excavations Bulletin*, published annually, and also available on www.excavations.ie
Note: The majority of sites are on private land and permission to visit them should be obtained from the owners.

The following abbreviations are used for publications:
Arch. Inv.   *Archaeological Inventory*
AI   *Archaeology Ireland*
ASCD   *Archaeological Survey of County Down* (1960)
JCHAS   *Journal Cork Historical and Archaeological Society*
JIA   *Journal of Irish Archaeology*
JRSAI   *Journal Royal Society of Antiquaries of Ireland*
MS I-VI   *Megalithic Survey of Ireland, volumes I-VI*
PBNHPS   *Proceedings of Belfast Natural History and Philosophical Society*
PRIA   *Proceedings of the Royal Irish Academy*
PSAMNI   *Preliminary Survey of the Ancient Monuments of Northern Ireland* (1940)
UJA   *Ulster Journal of Archaeology*

Sites to visit are listed by county, in alphabetical order.

Antrim
Ballylumford, ?passage tomb, D430016; *PSAMNI* 3; Hamlin (1983), plate 71.
Ballymacaldrack, court tomb, D022182; Evans, *UJA* 1 (1938), 59-68; Collins *UJA* 39 (1976), 1-7.
Ballymarlagh, court tomb, D141017; Davies, *UJA* 12 (1949), 26-42.
Browndod, court tomb, J205924; Davies and Evans, *PBNHPS* (1934-5), 70-87.
Craigs, court tomb, C979175; *PSAMNI* 22; Hamlin (1983), 69-70.
Craigs, passage tomb, C973172; Williams, *UJA* 50 (1987), 129-33.
Dunteige, wedge tomb, D323079; *PSAMNI*, 29.

Armagh
Annaghmare, court tomb, H905178; Waterman, *UJA* 28 (1965), 3-46.
Ballykeel, portal tomb, H995213; Collins, *UJA* 28 (1965), 47-70.
Ballymacdermot, court tomb, J066240; Collins and Wilson, *UJA* 27 (1964), 3-22.
Clontygora, court tomb, J098194; Davies and Paterson, *PBNHPS* 1 (1936–7), 20-42.
Slieve Gullion, passage tomb, J025203; Collins and Wilson, *UJA* 26 (1963), 19-40.

Carlow
Haroldstown, portal tomb, S900779; *Arch. Inv.* 2.
Kernanstown, portal tomb, S754768; *Arch. Inv.* 1.

Cavan
Aughrim, wedge tomb, H274211; *MS III* (Cv.14), now at Slieve Russell Hotel.
Burren, wedge tomb, H080351; *MS III* (Cv.5), 107-9.
Cohaw, court tomb, H644125; *MS III* (Cv.22) Kilbride-Jones; *PRIA* 54C (1951-2), 75-88.

Clare
Baur South, wedge tomb, M217000; *MS I* (C1.26).
Caheraphuca, wedge tomb, R392874; *MS I* (C1.80).
Derrynavahagh, wedge tomb, M180054; *MS I* (Cl.1).
Parknabinnia, court tomb, R260935; (C1.153), Jones, *JIA* (1998).
Parknabinnia, wedge tombs, R26493*; *MS I* (C1.66, 67), 54-55.
Poulaphuca, wedge tomb, M264017; *MS I* (C1.20).
Poulnabrone, portal tomb, M236003; (Cl.28), Lynch, *AI*, 2 (1988), 105-7.

Cork
Ahaglaslin, portal tomb, W307363; *MS IV* (Co.55).
Altar, wedge tomb, W858303; *MS IV* (Co.61); O'Brien (1999).
Arderawinny, portal tomb, V875307; *MS IV* (Co.62).
Inchincurka, wedge tomb, W233597; *MS IV* (Co.42).
Island, wedge tomb, W603908; O'Kelly, *JRSAI* 88 (1958), 1-23.
Keamcurravooly, wedge tomb, W136677; *MS IV* (Co.24).
Killickaforvane, passage tomb, V972221; O'Leary, *JCHAS* 94 (1989), 124-6.
Knockane, wedge tombs, W328645; *MS IV* (Co.30 and Co.31).
Labbacallee, wedge tomb, W772026; Leask and Price, *PRIA* 43C (1936), 77-101.
Ringarogy, passage tomb, W060288; Shee Twohig, *AI* (1995), 7-9.

Derry
Ballybriest, court tomb, H762886; Evans, *PRIA* 45C (1939), 1-12.
Boviel, wedge tomb, C730078; Herring and May, *UJA* 3 (1940), 41-55.
Knockoneill, court tomb, C819087; Flanagan, *UJA* 43 (1980), 9-14.
Tamnyrankin, court tomb, C838100; Herring, *PBNHPS* (1937), 43-9.

Tireighter, wedge tomb, C591019; *PSAMNI* (1940).
Tirnony, portal tomb, C840016; *PSAMNI* (1940), 309.

Donegal
Bavan, court tomb, G651755; Flanagan and Flanagan, *UJA* 29 (1966), 16-38 (Dg.12).
Farranmacbride, court tomb, G535854; *MS VI* (Dg.56).
Kilclooney More, portal tombs, G722967; *MS VI* (Dg.70).
Kilmonaster Middle, passage tombs, H 27*97*; *MS VI* p.181-2.
Malin More, court tomb, G519826; *MS VI* (Dg.95).
Malin More, six portal tombs, G500826; *MS VI* (Dg.91).
Shalwy, court tomb, G648753; *MS VI* (Dg.113).

Down
Audleystown, court tomb, J561503; Collins, *UJA* 17 (1954), 7-56; *UJA* 22 (1959), 21-5.
Ballynahatty, passage tomb and henge enclosure, J327677; Hartwell (1998).
Goward, court tomb, J236296; Davies and Evans, *PBNHPS* (1932-3), 90-105.
Goward, portal tomb, J243310; *ASCD* (1966), 79-80.
Greengraves, portal tomb, J445736; *ASCD* (1966), 79-80.
Kilfeaghan, portal tomb, J232153; Collins, *UJA* 22 (1959), 31-2.
Legananny, portal tomb, J288434; *ASCD* (1966), 81.

Dublin
Ballyedmonduff, wedge tomb, O185212; Ó Riordáin and de Valera, *PRIA* 55C (1952), 61-81.
Brenanstown, portal tomb, O229242; Corlett (1999), 103.
Kilmashogue, wedge tomb, O150244; Kilbride-Jones, *PRIA* 56C (1954), 461-79.
Kiltiernan, portal tomb, O197224; Corlett (1999), 106.

Fermanagh
Aghanaglack, court tomb, H098435; Davies, *JRSAI* 69 (1939), 21-38.
Ballyreagh, court tomb, H314503; Davies, *UJA* 5 (1942), 78-89.
Kiltierney, passage tomb, H217626; Foley in Hamlin and Lynn (editors) (1988), *Pieces of the Past*, HMSO, 24-6.

Galway
Crannagh, portal tomb, M426059; *MS III* (Ga.25).
Mweelin, court tomb, L755577; Gibbons, *AI* 2 (1989), (Ga.46).
Oghill, wedge tomb, L849098; *MS III* (Ga.21).
Sheeauns, court tomb, L624580; (Ga.62).

Kerry
Ballycarty, passage tomb, Q882123; Connolly (1999).
Ballyhoneen/Kilmore, wedge tomb, Q528080; *MS IV* (Ke.1); Cuppage 1986, 20-2.

Caherard, wedge tomb, Q390011; *MS IV* (Ke.3).
Cool East, wedge tomb, V376758; *MS IV* (Ke.11).
Coomatloukane, 4 wedge tombs, V50*60*; *MS IV* (Ke.17-20).
Drombohilly Upper, wedge tomb, V789606; Twohig, *Journal Kerry Archaeological and Historical Society* 19 (1986), 143-50 (Ke.26).

Kilkenny
Farnogue, court tomb, S601224; de Valera and Ó Nualláin, *JRSAI* 92 (1962), 117-23.
Kilmogue, portal tomb, S502281; Borlase (1897), 405-7.
Knockroe, passage tomb, S409312; O'Sullivan, *JRSAI* 123 (1993), 5-18.

Leitrim
Corracloona, court tomb, G996427; *MS III* (Le.18); Kilbride-Jones, *PRIA* 74C (1974), 171-82.
Kilnagarns Lower, court and wedge tombs, G936256; *MS III* (Le.27, 28); Corcoran, *JRSAI* 94 (1964), 177-95.

Limerick
Deerpark (Duntryleague), passage tomb; R778284; Ó Nualláin and Cody, *JRSAI* 117 (1987), 69-83.
Lough Gur, wedge tomb, R646402; *MS IV* (Li.4); Ó Riordáin and Ó h-Iceadha, *JRSAI* 85 (1955), 34-50.

Longford
Aghnacliff, portal tomb, N263885; *MS III* (Lf.3), 87.
Melkagh, portal tomb, N161879; *MS III* (Lf.1), 87; Cooney, *PRIA* 97C (1997), 195-244.

Louth
Aghnaskeagh, court tomb, J076136; Evans, *County Louth Archaeological Journal* 9 (1937), 1-18.
Aghnaskeagh, portal tomb, J075137; Evans, *County Louth Archaeological Journal* 8 (1933-6), 234-55.
Paddock, wedge tomb, O049830; *Arch. Inv.* 34.
Proleek, portal tomb, J082110; *Arch. Inv.* 35.
Proleek, wedge tomb, J083110; *Arch. Inv.* 35.
Townleyhall, passage tomb, O023758; Eogan, *JRSAI* 93 (1963), 37-81.

Mayo
Alliemore, court tomb, L761738; *MS II* (Ma.89).
Ballyglass, court tomb, G097381; *MS II* (Ma.13); Ó Nualláin, *JRSAI* 102 (1972), 2-11.
Ballyglass, court tomb, G098379; *MS II* (Ma.14); Ó Nualláin, *PRIA* 93C (1998), 125-75.
Behy, court tomb, G050405; *MS II* (Ma.3).
Carbad More, court tomb, G181326; *MS II* (Ma.36).

Carrowkilleen, court tomb, G083168; *MS II* (Ma.52).
Rathlacken, court tomb, G166387; (Ma.116), Byrne, *Excavations Bulletin* (1990, 1992, 1993).
Srahwee, wedge tomb, L795745; *MS II* (Ma.91), 82.

Meath
Castleboy (Tara), passage tomb, N920597; Herity (1974), 252-3 (list of finds).
Dowth, passage tomb, O023737; O'Kelly and O'Kelly, *PRIA* 83C (1983), 135-90.
Fourknocks, passage tomb, O108619; Hartnett, *PRIA* 58C (1957), 197-277.
Knowth, passage tombs, N996734; Eogan (1986).
Loughcrew, passage tombs, N586775 (centre hill); Shee Twohig (1981).
Newgrange, passage tombs, O007727; O'Kelly (1982).

Monaghan
Calliagh, wedge tomb, H638267; *Arch. Inv.* 1.
Carn, court tomb, H611258; *Arch. Inv.* 1.
Lisnadarragh, wedge tomb, H725077; *Arch. Inv.* 1.

Roscommon
Drumanone, portal tomb, G768024; *MS III* (Ro.3); Topp, *Bulletin of Institute of Archaeology, University of London* (1962), 38-46.
Scregg, passage tomb, M528552; *MS III*, 142.
Usna, wedge tomb, G887016; *MS III* (Ro.4).

Sligo
Carrickglass, portal tomb, G795157; *MS V* (Sl.102); Borlase (1897), 184-5.
Carrowkeel-Keshcorran, passage tombs, G744116 to G759117; Macalister *et al*, *PRIA* 29C (1912), 311-47.
Carrowmore, passage tombs, G662334 (Listoghil, centre tomb); Bergh (1995); Burenhult (2001).
Creevykeel, court tomb, G719545; (Sl.5), Hencken, *JRSAI* 69 (1939), 53-98.
Deerpark/Magheraghanarush, court tomb, G751367; *MS V* (Sl.47).
Knocknarea, passage tomb, G626346; Bergh (1995).

Tipperary
Baurnadomeeny, wedge tomb, R846603; (Ti.6), O'Kelly *JCHAS* 65 (1960), 85-115.
Loughbrack, wedge tomb, R906592; *MS IV* (Ti.11), 90.
Shanballyedmond, court tomb, R844588; (Ti.7), O'Kelly, *JCHAS* 63 (1958), 37-72.
Shrough, passage tomb, R841306; Ó Nualláin and Cody, *JRSAI* 117 (1987), 69-83.

Tyrone
Balix Lower, court tomb, H483963; Lynch, *UJA* 29 (1966), 39-42.
Ballyrenan, portal tomb, H373832; Davies, *JRSAI* 67 (1937), 89-100.

Clady Haliday, court tomb, H343886; Davies and Radford, *PBNHPS* (1935-6), 76-85.
Creggandevesky, court tomb, H646750; Foley in Hamlin and Lynn (editors) (1988), *Pieces of the Past*, HMSO, 3-5.
Knockmany, passage tomb, H547558; Shee Twohig (1981), 203-5.
Loughash, (Cashelbane) wedge tomb, C516013; Davies and Mullen, *JRSAI* 70 (1940), 143-63.
Loughash, (Giant's Grave) wedge tomb, C483008; Davies, *UJA* 2 (1939), 254-62.
Sesskilgreen, passage tomb, H604584; Shee Twohig (1981), 202-3.

Waterford
Ballynamona Lower, court tomb, X287835; Powell, *JRSAI* 68 (1938), 260-71.
Carriglong, passage tomb, S590049; Powell, *JCHAS* 46 (1941), 55-62.
Gaulstown, portal tomb, S540062; *Arch. Inv.* 2.
Harristown, passage tomb, S676040; Hawkes, *JRSAI* 71 (1941), 130-47.
Knockeen, portal tomb, S575064; *Arch. Inv.* 2.

Wexford
Ballybrittas, portal tomb, S927316; *Arch. Inv.* 1.

Wicklow
Baltinglass Hill, passage tomb, S885892; Walshe, *PRIA* 46 (1941), 221-36.
Carrig, wedge tomb, N944121; *Arch. Inv.* 6.
Moylisha, wedge tomb, S930675; Ó hIceadha, *JRSAI* 76 (1946), 119-28.
Scurlocksleap, (Seefin) passage tomb, O073162; *Arch. Inv.* 5.

10
Further reading

References to individual sites are given in abbreviated form after the site entry in Chapter 9.

Bergh, S. 1995. *Landscape of the Monuments.* Stockholm: Riksantikvarieämbetet Arkeologiska Undersöknigar.

Borlase, W. C. 1897. *The Dolmens of Ireland.* London: Chapman & Hall.

Burenhult, G. 2001. *The Illustrated Guide to the Megalithic Cemetery of Carrowmore, Co. Sligo.* Tjörnap: Burenhult.

Caulfield, S. 1983. 'The Neolithic Settlement of North Connaught' in T. Reeves-Smyth and F. Hamond (editors). *Landscape Archaeology in Ireland.* Oxford: British Archaeological Reports, 195-216.

Chart, D. A. (editor), 1940. *A Preliminary Survey of the Ancient Monuments of Northern Ireland.* Belfast: HMSO.

Cody, E. 2002. *Survey of the Megalithic Tombs of Ireland. Volume VI, County Donegal.* Dublin: Stationery Office.

Connolly, M. 1999. *Discovering the Neolithic in County Kerry: A Passage Tomb at Ballycarty.* Bray: Wordwell.

Cooney, G. 1983. 'Megalithic Tombs in Their Environmental Setting, a Perspective' in T. Reeves-Smyth and F. Hamond (editors). *Landscape Archaeology in Ireland.* Oxford: British Archaeological Reports, 179-94.

Cooney, G. 2000. *Neolithic Landscapes of Ireland.* London: Routledge.

Corlett, C. 1999. *Antiquities of Old Rathdown.* Bray: Wordwell.

Cuppage, J. 1986. *Corca Dhuibhne. Dingle Peninsula Archaeological Survey.* Dingle: Oidhreacht Corca Dhuibne.

de Valera, R. 1960. 'The Court Cairns of Ireland'. *Proceedings of the Royal Irish Academy* 60C, 9-140.

de Valera, R., and Ó Nualláin, S. 1961. *Survey of the Megalithic Tombs of Ireland. Volume I, County Clare.* Dublin: Stationery Office.

de Valera, R., and Ó Nualláin, S. 1964. *Survey of the Megalithic Tombs of Ireland. Volume II, County Mayo.* Dublin: Stationery Office.

de Valera, R., and Ó Nualláin, S. 1972. *Survey of the Megalithic Tombs of Ireland. Volume III, Counties Galway, Roscommon, Leitrim, Longford, Westmeath, Laoighis, Offaly, Kildare, Cavan.* Dublin: Stationery Office.

de Valera, R., and Ó Nualláin, S. 1982. *Survey of the Megalithic Tombs of Ireland. Volume IV, Counties Cork, Kerry, Limerick, Tipperary.*

Dublin: Stationery Office.

Eogan, G. 1986. *Knowth and the Passage Tombs of Ireland.* London: Thames & Hudson.

Eogan, G., and Roche, H. 1997. *Excavations at Knowth 2.* Dublin: Royal Irish Academy.

Gibbons, M., and Higgins, J. 1988. 'Connemara's Emerging Prehistory'. *Archaeology Ireland* 2, 63-6.

Hamlin, A. (editor). 1983. *Historic Monuments of Northern Ireland: An Introduction and Guide.* Belfast: HMSO.

Harbison, P. 1992. *Guide to the National and Historic Monuments of Ireland.* Dublin: Gill & MacMillan.

Hartwell, B. 1998. 'The Ballynahatty Complex' in A. Gibson and D. D. A. Simpson (editors). *Prehistoric Ritual and Religion.* Stroud: Sutton, 32-44.

Herity, M. 1964. 'The Finds from Irish Portal Dolmens'. *Journal of the Royal Society of Antiquaries of Ireland* 94, 123-44.

Herity, M. 1974. *Irish Passage Graves.* Dublin: Irish University Press.

Herity, M. 1982. 'Irish Decorated Neolithic Pottery'. *Proceedings of the Royal Irish Academy* 82C, 247-404.

Herity, M. 1987. 'The Finds from Irish Court Tombs'. *Proceedings of the Royal Irish Academy* 87C, 103-281.

Hurl, D. 2001. 'The Excavation of a Wedge Tomb at Ballybriest, County Londonderry'. *Ulster Journal of Archaeology* 60, 9-31.

Jones, C. 1998. 'The Discovery and Dating of the Prehistoric Landscape of Roughan Hill in Co. Clare'. *Journal of Irish Archaeology* 9, 27-44.

Lynch, F. M. 1997. *Megalithic Tombs and Long Barrows in Britain.* Princes Risborough: Shire.

Mallory, J., and McNeill, T. 1991. *The Archaeology of Ulster from Colonization to Plantation.* Belfast: Institute of Irish Studies.

O'Brien, W. 1999. *Megalithic Tombs in Coastal South-West Ireland.* Galway: Department of Archaeology, National University of Ireland, Galway.

O'Connell, M., and Molloy, K. 2001. 'Farming and Woodland Dynamics in Ireland during the Neolithic'. *Proceedings of the Royal Irish Academy* 101B, 99-128.

O'Kelly, C. 1978. *Illustrated Guide to Newgrange and the Other Boyne Monuments.* Cork: C. O'Kelly.

O'Kelly, M. J. 1981. 'The Megalithic Tombs of Ireland' in J. D. Evans, B. Cunliffe and C. Renfrew (editors). *Antiquity and Man; Essays in Honour of Glyn Daniel.* London: Thames & Hudson, 177-90.

O'Kelly, M. J. 1982. *Newgrange: Archaeology, Art and Legend.* London: Thames & Hudson.

O'Kelly, M. J. 1988. *Early Ireland: An Introduction to Irish Prehistory.*

Cambridge: Cambridge University Press.

Ó Nualláin, S. 1983. 'Irish Portal Tombs; Topography, Siting and Distribution'. *Journal of the Royal Society of Antiquaries of Ireland* 113, 75-105.

Ó Nualláin, S. 1989. *Survey of the Megalithic Tombs of Ireland. Volume V, Co. Sligo.* Dublin: Stationery Office.

Powell, T. G. E. 1973. 'Excavations of a Megalithic Chambered Tomb at Dyffryn Ardudwy, Merioneth, Wales'. *Archaeologia* 104, 1-50.

Ryan, M. (editor). 1997. *Irish Archaeology Illustrated.* Dublin: Country House.

Shee Twohig, E. 1981. *The Megalithic Art of Western Europe.* Oxford: Clarendon Press.

Stout, G. 2002. *Newgrange and the Bend of the Boyne.* Cork: Cork University Press.

Waddell, J. 1998. *The Prehistoric Archaeology of Ireland.* Galway: Galway University Press.

Walsh, P. 1995. 'Structure and Deposition in Irish Wedge Tombs: An Open and Shut Case?' in J. Waddell and E. Shee Twohig (editors). *Ireland in the Bronze Age.* Dublin: Stationery Office, 113-27.

Woodman, P. C. 2000. 'Getting Back to Basics: Transitions to Farming in Ireland and Britain' in T. Douglas Price (editor). *Europe's First Farmers.* Cambridge: Cambridge University Press, 219-60.

Index